CONTENTS

1.	Counting the People of God	5
2.	Purity & Presence	13
3.	Complaints & Quail	21
4.	Rebellion in the Camp	29
5.	Tests of Authority	37
6.	Sin, Water, & Leadership	45
7.	The Bronze Serpent	53
8.	Balaam & the Blessings of God	61
9.	A New Generation	69
10.	Sacrifices, Vows, & Vengeance	77
11.	The Transjordan Tribes	85
12.	Remembering the Journey	93
13.	Boundaries & Inheritance	101

NUMBERS
FROM START2FINISH

MICHAEL WHITWORTH

© 2025 by Start2Finish

All rights reserved. No part of this publication may be reproduced, stored in a retrieval system, or transmitted in any form or by any means without the prior written permission of the author. The only exception is brief quotations in printed reviews.

ISBN 978-1-941972-86-1

Published by Start2Finish
Bend, Oregon 97702
start2finish.org

Printed in the United States of America

Unless otherwise noted, all Scripture quotations are from The Holy Bible, English Standard Version®, copyright © 2001 by Crossway Bibles, a publishing ministry of Good News Publishers. Used by permission. All rights reserved.

Cover Design: Evangela Creative

1

COUNTING THE PEOPLE OF GOD

NUMBERS 1-4

> **Objective:** To show that God's people thrive when their lives and service follow his divine order.

INTRODUCTION

Nothing tests order like moving day. No matter how carefully you plan, something always gets misplaced—a box of dishes goes missing, the tool you need is buried under a mountain of bubble wrap, and everyone suddenly has a different opinion about where the couch should go. Moving chaos exposes whether there's any real structure behind the plan. Israel's "moving day" came at Mount Sinai. After a year in the shadow of the mountain, it was time to pack up camp, carry the tabernacle, and march toward the Promised Land. But before the first trumpet sounded, God gave detailed instructions. He wasn't wasting time—he was building order.

Numbers 1-4 might read like a census report, but beneath the numbers beats a message about divine organization. God turns a crowd of former slaves into a coordinated people. Every tribe receives a banner, every family a place, every Levite a task. Israel's geography becomes theology— God in the center, his people arranged around him. It's a vivid reminder that holiness and order go hand in hand. The same God who spoke the cosmos into symmetry now brings structure to his covenant people. Without order, their journey would collapse into chaos. Before Israel could conquer Canaan, they had to first learn to follow their Commander's design.

EXAMINATION

The census commanded (1:1-19)

The book of Numbers opens not with adventure but arithmetic. From the very first verse, God demonstrates that even counting his people is sacred business. "The Lord spoke to Moses in the wilderness of Sinai, in the tent of meeting" (1:1). The setting links this book to Exodus and Leviticus—Israel was still camped at Mount Sinai, roughly a year after leaving Egypt. The covenant had been ratified, the tabernacle constructed, and the priesthood consecrated. Before they march toward Canaan, God commanded a census.

The book's title in Hebrew is *bemidbar*, "in the wilderness." It captures both the geography and the theology of the book. Israel was between redemption and promise—delivered from Egypt but not yet home. To move forward, the nation had be put in order. God is a God of structure, not chaos. He arranges his people as carefully as he arranged the stars in heaven.

Moses and Aaron were instructed to count "all in Israel who are able to go to war, every man by his clans, by his fathers' houses" (1:2). The census was not merely administrative; it was preparatory for conquest. This generation was called to advance God's promises through obedience and battle. Each tribe's men, twenty years old and upward, were numbered for potential military service. Leaders from each tribe were named to assist—showing that God values shared leadership and accountability.

Even here, in what might appear as tedious lists, there is theology. Israel's identity was corporate, not individualistic. Each man belonged to a family, each family to a tribe, each tribe to a nation under God's rule. The structure itself declared: God's people are not a mob; they are a movement. The wilderness would expose whether this movement was disciplined or disordered.

The tribes numbered (1:20-54)

The census proceeded tribe by tribe. Judah led the count with 74,600 men—already hinting at its prominence among the tribes and foreshadowing its royal destiny. The total of 603,550 men (excluding the Levites) gives the impression of a mighty host. The promise to Abraham—that his descendants would be as numerous as the stars—had come true. What began with one elderly couple now filled a camp the size of a small nation.

Modern readers often stumble over the precision of these numbers. Some scholars suggest they symbolize completeness rather than literal totals, but the text treats them as factual tallies. The point is not the mathematics but the message: God's blessings can be counted. Every tribe, every family, every name matters to him. No one is lost in the crowd.

Notice the symmetry of the list. Each tribe contributed to the whole, but none stood alone. The repetition of "according to their clans, by their fathers' houses" reinforces the sense of order. Israel was not a random assembly; it was a divinely arranged community. The book's opening chapter functions like a roll call of faithfulness—God called, and the people answered.

The exclusion of the Levites in verse 47 introduces an important theme: holiness requires separation. The Levites were exempt from the military census because their calling was priestly, not martial. Their service in the tabernacle represents another kind of warfare—the defense of holiness against impurity. The text ends with an orderly summary: "Thus did the people of Israel; they did according to all that the Lord commanded Moses" (1:54). For now, obedience reigned.

The camp arranged (2:1–34)

If chapter 1 numbered the people, chapter 2 organizes them. The Lord directed Moses and Aaron to assign each tribe its place around the tabernacle. God dwelt in the center, symbolizing that Israel's life revolved around his presence. Every tent faced the sanctuary. The camp was both theological and practical architecture—a visible sermon about life oriented toward God.

The arrangement formed a vast square with the tabernacle in the middle. The east side hosted Judah, Issachar, and Zebulun—collectively the largest and most prominent formation, fitting for the tribe that would one day lead the nation. To the south stood Reuben, Simeon, and Gad; to the west, Ephraim, Manasseh, and Benjamin; to the north, Dan, Asher, and Naphtali. The Levites camped nearest the tabernacle, forming a protective buffer between the sanctuary and the rest of the tribes.

This symmetry was not mere logistics. The camp reflected heaven's order. In Ezekiel's vision, angelic beings surround God's throne in similar formation. Later Jewish tradition imagined each standard bearing its tribal symbol—a lion for Judah, a man for Reuben, an ox for Ephraim, and an eagle for Dan. Revelation 4 borrows the same imagery to depict the heavenly throne room. Thus, even Israel's camp foreshadowed divine realities.

God's order fosters unity and purpose. When the cloud lifted, signaling travel, each tribe moved in sequence, not confusion. When it rested, each returned to its appointed place. In an age where everyone does what is right in his own eyes, Numbers 2 stands as a rebuke. God's people thrive under structure. His presence in the center of the camp reminded them—and us—that holiness requires both proximity and order.

The Levites set apart (3:1–51)

Chapter 3 focuses on those who serve closest to the tabernacle: the Levites. Their calling was rooted in substitution. Instead of every firstborn Israelite belonging to God, he claimed the entire tribe of Levi in their place (3:12–13). This exchange kept Israel's redemption ever before them—the memory of Egypt's final plague and the price of deliverance. The Levites embodied that redemption through perpetual service.

Aaron's sons are named—Nadab, Abihu, Eleazar, and Ithamar. The narrative recalls Nadab and Abihu's fatal sin (v. 4), reminding readers that nearness to God demands reverence. The Levites assisted the priests but did not intrude upon their duties. Each clan within Levi—Gershon, Kohath, and Merari—was assigned specific responsibilities. Gershon handled the tabernacle curtains and coverings; Kohath managed the sacred furniture; Merari cared for the structural elements. Even when it comes to holy service, God organizes.

The census of Levites (from one month old and up) totaled 22,000. Correspondingly, the number of Israel's firstborn males was 22,273. The 273 excess are redeemed by a payment of five shekels each—a vivid illustration of substitutionary redemption. Every number told a story: God's holiness cannot be approached casually, and his people are ransomed by precise atonement.

This chapter also highlights God's grace in administration. Service was distributed according to ability and lineage. No clan could claim superiority, and no task was insignificant. Whether carrying sockets or tending incense, each Levite contributed to the nation's worship. In a community ordered by divine wisdom, every role had dignity.

The Levites counted (4:1–49)

If chapter 3 identifies who the Levites were, chapter 4 specifies what they did. Here, the focus narrows to those between thirty and fifty years old—men in the prime of strength—tasked with transporting the tabernacle's holy items. The Kohathites carried the most sacred objects: the ark, table, lampstand, and altars. These had to be covered by Aaron and his sons before the camp moved. The detailed wrapping—blue cloth for the ark, scarlet for the table, purple for the altar—turned packing into liturgy. Every color and covering reinforced reverence.

The Gershonites handled the curtains and ropes; the Merarites bore the boards and pillars. Each group was supervised by one of Aaron's sons and assigned by name. The refrain "according to all that the Lord commanded Moses" underscored that divine order governed even the logistics of moving camp.

This may seem mundane, but it reveals a profound truth: worship and work belong together. God's holiness extends to organization, labor, and timing. Israel's mobility demanded coordination; holiness demands precision. When the sanctuary was disassembled and reassembled according to God's pattern, his people learned that obedience is not confined to ritual—it includes rhythm.

The chapter closes with another total: 8,580 Levites eligible for service. Nothing was left to chance. God counted because he cared. His order sustained Israel's worship and ensured their journey continued without chaos.

Together, these four chapters display a portrait of divine organization. God's people were counted, arranged, and commissioned. The wilderness would soon test their order, but the opening act of Numbers establishes that movement without structure leads to confusion. God's presence calls for both reverence and readiness.

APPLICATION

1. God values order among his people

The first four chapters of Numbers show that organization is not a bureaucratic nuisance but a reflection of God's nature. The God who spoke galaxies into existence also arranged the tribes of Israel around his presence. When his people are structured well, they reveal something about him to the world—his stability, his clarity, and his peace. Churches that ignore order often slide into confusion or conflict, while those that honor biblical patterns of leadership, worship, and service experience harmony and fruitfulness. This isn't about rigid control but spiritual health. When God assigns roles and boundaries, it's for the good of his people. Divine order protects unity and promotes mission. Every list, name, and instruction in Numbers whispers that God's work flourishes best in an environment shaped by his wisdom and design.

2. Everyone has a role to fulfill

Israel's camp functioned like a living organism. Every man had a task; every tribe had a place. No one was left idle, and no one was unnecessary. God designed it that way. The same principle applies to the church today. Paul described believers as parts of one body—different gifts, same purpose (Rom. 12:4–8). Some lead or teach, others comfort or serve, and together they make God's presence visible in the world. When members neglect their role, the body limps; when all work together, the body thrives. Numbers reminds us that even the least glamorous duties—carrying poles, folding curtains, guarding entrances—are acts of worship when done faithfully. The kingdom doesn't advance through celebrity or spectacle but through countless Christians quietly fulfilling their God-given roles with excellence and humility.

3. Holiness requires structure

God's holiness demanded boundaries. The Levites surrounded the tabernacle not because God was distant but because his presence was dangerous to approach carelessly. Their organized service ensured that holiness could dwell safely among the people. The church today also requires spiritual order. Our worship must be guided by Scripture, not preference; our leadership must follow the New Testament pattern of shepherds, servants, and saints working together. When we discard structure in the name of freedom, we risk turning reverence into chaos. True holiness isn't spontaneous disorder—it's joyful obedience to God's pattern. Israel's camp teaches that form and function matter. When the community honors God's commands, the result isn't rigidity but glory. Structure becomes the trellis on which holiness grows and blossoms.

4. God's precision reveals his care

To human eyes, the censuses and measurements of Numbers may seem tedious, but to God, every detail tells a story of love. He knew the exact number of warriors, firstborn sons, and Levites because each represented a person he valued. His numbering wasn't impersonal—it was intimate. In the same way, Jesus spoke of a Father who knows the number of hairs on our heads. Divine order is not cold accounting; it's careful attention. When God arranges our lives, establishes boundaries, or even delays our progress, it's not because he's indifferent—it's because he's involved. The God who organized Israel's camp still orders our steps. His precision is an expression of personal affection, ensuring that nothing in our journey is wasted or overlooked.

CONCLUSION

Numbers opens with roll calls and marching orders, but beneath the logistics lies a lesson for life: God's people flourish when they live by his design. The census, camp, and priestly duties were not mere formalities—they were acts of faith. Israel's order reflected their trust that God knew where each person belonged. In the church today, that same principle still holds. When believers honor God's structure in worship, leadership, and daily service, harmony replaces confusion and purpose replaces drift. The God who arranged the wilderness camp still arranges our lives. His order is not restriction; it is direction—guiding us safely toward the promise he has prepared.

REFLECTION

1. What does Israel's census reveal about God's character and his concern for order?

2. How does seeing the camp arranged around the tabernacle shape your view of God's presence today?

3. In what ways do you see God's organization reflected in creation and the church?

4. Why is it important to recognize both structure and relationship in serving God?

5. How might viewing your own role in the church through Numbers 1–4 change your attitude toward service?

6. What do these chapters teach about the connection between obedience and readiness for mission?

DISCUSSION

1. How can modern churches balance flexibility with faithfulness to God's design?

2. What dangers arise when a congregation loses respect for spiritual structure and leadership?

3. In what ways can "divine order" bring peace and unity in times of conflict?

4. How does the Levites' organization help us understand reverence and boundaries in worship today?

5. What practical lessons about teamwork and delegation can church leaders learn from Moses and Aaron?

6. How do these chapters prepare Israel—and us—for movement toward God's promises?

2

PURITY & PRESENCE

NUMBERS 5:1–10:10

Objective: To show that purity is essential preparation for experiencing and carrying God's presence.

INTRODUCTION

A surgeon once remarked that the most important part of his job isn't cutting—it's cleaning. Before a single incision is made, he scrubs his hands, sanitizes instruments, and ensures the environment is sterile. One lapse in hygiene can invite infection and threaten life. Precision saves, but purity protects. The same principle governed Israel's preparation at Mt. Sinai. Before they could march, God had to cleanse. Before they could move, God had to make them holy.

Numbers 5–10 reads like a manual for spiritual sanitation. The people were purified from disease, defilement, and moral disorder. Sin was confessed, restitution made, and relationships restored. Nazirites dedicated themselves to holiness, priests pronounced blessing, Levites were consecrated, lamps were lit, and trumpets prepared. Every detail communicates one central truth: purity is the pathway to presence. God will dwell only among a clean people, not because he is cruel, but because he is holy.

These chapters reveal that holiness isn't about scrubbing hands—it's about cleansing hearts. God wanted more than a well-organized camp; he desired a community that reflected his character. The order of the camp, the brightness of the lamps, and the rhythm of the trumpets all proclaimed the same message: God moves with the pure. Before Israel could conquer the wilderness, they had to be conquered by holiness. Only then could they walk with the God who dwelt in their midst.

EXAMINATION

Purity in the camp (5:1–31)

God had ordered Israel's army (chs. 1–4). Now he ordered its soul. Numbers 5 shifts from logistics to life, insisting that purity is the condition for divine presence. The camp was not merely a military formation—it was a sanctuary on the move. The Lord instructed Moses to "put out of the camp everyone who is leprous or has a discharge or is unclean through contact with the dead" (5:2). These laws were not arbitrary or heartless; they embodied holiness in visible form. The holy God intended to dwell among his people, and impurity—whether ceremonial, moral, or relational—could not coexist with his glory.

These commands extended Leviticus' purity code into the geography of Israel's daily life. The camp itself became an outer court of the tabernacle, and every tent participated in holiness. Removal of the unclean was not rejection but mercy: isolation prevented contagion and preserved the sanctity of God's presence. When the text repeats "so that they do not defile their camp, in the midst of which I dwell" (5:3), the emphasis is unmistakable. God's presence is both privilege and peril.

The following verses (5:5–10) shift from ritual impurity to moral impurity. Theft, deceit, and broken trust defiled the community just as surely as disease. The offender had to confess and make restitution, adding a fifth of the value to demonstrate sincerity. Sin always costs more than we think. These instructions show that holiness is relational, not just ritual. To be clean before God means to live rightly with others.

The final portion of the chapter (5:11–31) details the ordeal of the suspected adulteress, one of the most curious laws in the Torah. It has provoked modern discomfort, but understood in context, it reveals divine justice and protection. In a patriarchal culture where jealousy could easily turn violent, God provided a measured, priest-supervised process to resolve suspicion. The "bitter water" ritual placed the outcome in God's hands, not human anger. The innocent woman would be vindicated; the guilty would face divine judgment. This section reinforces the central concern of the entire chapter: purity safeguarded the camp's unity. Whether the issue was disease, dishonesty, or infidelity, holiness had to be guarded because God dwells among his people.

Dedication and blessing (6:1–27)

If chapter 5 described enforced purity, chapter 6 celebrates voluntary purity. The Nazirite vow invited ordinary Israelites to pursue extraordinary devotion. Anyone—man or woman—could take the vow to "separate himself to the Lord" for a season (6:2). In a community where priestly holiness was restricted to one tribe, this vow democratized sanctity. God's presence was not reserved for clergy; any Israelite could draw near through disciplined consecration.

Three visible signs marked the vow: abstaining from wine, avoiding corpses, and allowing the hair to grow uncut. Each symbolized devotion. Wine represented earthly joy; the Nazirite surrendered even legitimate pleasures to focus wholly on God. Avoiding death kept the Nazirite ritually clean, echoing the priestly standard. Uncut hair was a public declaration of separation—a visible testimony that one's strength and identity belonged to the Lord. Samson and Samuel later embody this calling in permanent form.

When the period of dedication ended, the Nazirite offered a burnt offering, sin offering, and peace offering (6:13–21). The ritual's complexity reminds us that consecration requires atonement; purity depends on grace.

This chapter concludes with the Aaronic blessing (6:22–27), one of the most radiant texts in the Old Testament. After all the cleansing, vows, and offerings, God himself spoke words of blessing: "The Lord bless you and keep you… the Lord make his face to shine upon you." The sequence is profound. Purity prepares the way for presence, and presence results in peace. The shining face of God reverses the curse of Eden; fellowship replaces fear. In a book filled with numbers and names, this benediction sings of divine intimacy. The God who demands holiness now delights to bless his holy people.

Offerings and obedience (7:1-89)

Chapter 7, the longest in Numbers, recounts the dedication offerings for the tabernacle. Twelve tribes brought identical gifts over twelve days—silver plates and basins, gold bowls, grain, incense, and livestock for sacrifice. The repetitiveness seems tedious until we recognize its theological purpose: God's presence invites equal participation. No tribe received preferential treatment; every group approached God through the same pattern. The repetition also mirrors the steady rhythm of worship. Obedience is not creative improvisation but faithful repetition of what God commands.

The offerings corresponded to the structure of the altar and tabernacle described earlier. In this way, Israel's generosity mirrored God's design. The people gave according to the pattern revealed, reinforcing the central message of Numbers 5-10—holiness and order go hand in hand. This meticulous account also fulfilled Exodus 40's anticipation that the tabernacle would be "set up and consecrated." Numbers 7 marks the moment that structure became sanctuary.

The chapter concludes with an extraordinary statement: "When Moses went into the tent of meeting to speak with the Lord, he heard the voice speaking to him from above the mercy seat" (7:89). After long chapters of regulation, this verse is electric. God spoke. Purity had produced presence. The same voice that had thundered from Sinai now whispered from the tabernacle's heart. The order, offerings, and obedience had achieved their goal: fellowship between heaven and earth.

Light, consecration, and guidance (8:1-9:23)

The next section turns from offerings to illumination. Aaron was commanded to light the seven lamps of the lampstand (8:1-4), ensuring that the tabernacle continually glowed with divine light. This is no mere interior design choice. The menorah's light symbolized revelation and direction. God's holiness does not merely separate—it enlightens. Purity makes vision possible; sin clouds perception.

The Levites' purification (8:5-26) parallels priestly ordination in Leviticus. They were sprinkled, shaved, washed, and offered to God as a living wave offering. Every act dramatized that ministry requires cleansing before service. Their substitution for Israel's firstborn (8:16-19) recalls the Passover, connecting holiness to redemption once again. These men stood as living reminders that deliverance demands dedication.

Numbers 9 extends this principle through the celebration of the first anniversary Passover (9:1–14). It's a remarkable scene: a year after leaving Egypt, Israel still ate unleavened bread in the wilderness. The ceremony anchored them in memory while preparing them for movement. God graciously provided a "second Passover" for those who were unclean or on a journey, showing that holiness is not legal rigidity but relational grace. The entire nation, whether on time or delayed, shared in the same redemptive story.

The second half of Numbers 9 (vv. 15–23) shifts from purification to presence. The cloud and fire appeared again as the visual sign of God's indwelling glory. When the cloud lifted, Israel set out; when it settled, they encamped. Whether the stay lasted a day or a year, they moved only when God moved. This image encapsulates the entire theology of Numbers: purity enables guidance, and guidance sustains faith.

Trumpets and readiness (10:1–10)

The section closes with a brief but powerful paragraph describing two silver trumpets. Crafted from hammered silver, these instruments organized Israel's movements—summoning assemblies, signaling travel, and even announcing war. Their tones distinguished between gathering and going, between worship and warfare. Through them, divine order becomes audible. Every trumpet blast declared that Israel marched by command, not by impulse.

In festival seasons, the trumpets accompanied offerings "as a reminder before your God" (10:10). Purified worshipers now lived in harmony with God's voice. The same Lord who spoke from Sinai now communicated through ordered signals within the camp.

With the trumpets ready, the nation stood poised for departure. The first ten chapters of Numbers have transformed a redeemed rabble into a consecrated community. They were clean, organized, and responsive. God had numbered them, purified them, blessed them, illuminated them, and given them his presence. The narrative rhythm—command, obedience, blessing—builds toward movement. Israel was finally ready to journey with God through the wilderness.

The theology is unmistakable: *purity leads to presence*. God does not dwell among chaos. Before he guides his people, he cleanses them; before he moves them, he molds them. From the outcast at the camp's edge to the priest before the altar, everyone's holiness matters because God's holiness fills the camp. The book of Numbers begins not with travel but with transformation. By the time the first trumpet sounds, Israel had learned that order is the prelude to intimacy, and purity is the price of presence.

APPLICATION

1. God's presence requires purity

Before Israel could march, they had to be made clean. Every removal, ritual, and restriction in Numbers 5-10 drove home this point: the holy God will not dwell among an unholy people. Purity was not optional housekeeping; it was the condition for fellowship. Today, the church still lives by this truth. God's Spirit indwells a people redeemed by Christ's blood and called to moral and spiritual holiness. We cannot seek God's presence while tolerating the filth of sin in our hearts or the divisions of sin in our communities. The wilderness camp teaches us that God's nearness is both a gift and a responsibility. When Christians pursue purity—of thought, speech, motive, and worship—they make room for the presence that transforms. Holiness is not how we earn God's favor; it is how we enjoy it.

2. Discipline opens the way to devotion

The Nazirite vow shows that holiness is a choice of focus, not fanaticism. Any Israelite could voluntarily embrace deeper dedication by abstaining from certain pleasures to cultivate intimacy with God. That pattern still matters. A holy life doesn't happen by accident; it's formed through discipline. Prayer, fasting, service, and sacrifice are not drudgery but devotion. The Nazirite's long hair and abstinence weren't strange quirks—they were visible reminders that true joy flows from consecration. In our age of indulgence, restraint feels radical. Yet believers who practice holy habits experience God's presence more vividly. Discipline doesn't replace grace; it channels it. Just as a Nazirite's vow ended in celebration and blessing, so our disciplined devotion prepares us to receive the fullness of God's favor. Spiritual order always precedes spiritual encounter.

3. Obedience creates harmony among God's people

Chapter 7's repetition—the same offering repeated twelve times—illustrates a principle as relevant now as it was then: unity grows through shared obedience. When every tribe followed the same pattern, competition disappeared and harmony reigned. Worship became a unifying act, not a tribal performance. The same is true in the church today. Congregations flourish when members follow Scripture's pattern for worship, leadership, and service instead of inventing their own. Obedience may seem dull compared to innovation, but God delights in faithfulness. Every act of obedience—whether singing, giving, serving, or forgiving—builds communal harmony and invites God's voice into our midst. God's presence fills a people who are orderly, submissive, and united.

4. Purity prepares us for mission

The purification laws, the consecration of the Levites, and the trumpets of chapter 10 all build toward one goal: readiness to move. Israel's cleansing was not an end in itself; it was preparation to journey with God. Holiness equips God's people for service. Churches often long for revival or growth without realizing that renewal must precede momentum. We cannot carry God's presence into the world unless we first let him cleanse our hearts. Purity fuels mission. Just as the cloud and fire directed Israel's every move, the Spirit leads a sanctified church into fruitful work. Before we march into battle or ministry, we must be made clean. The God who guides us is the same God who purifies us. Holiness is not a hindrance to mission—it is its engine.

CONCLUSION

Before Israel could journey, God cleansed their camp. Before they could move, he purified their hearts. Numbers 5–10 reminds us that holiness is not a formality—it's a foundation. Purity is the precondition for God's presence. Every law, vow, offering, and trumpet prepared the people to walk with him. In the same way, Christians cannot carry God's presence into a corrupt world without first being cleansed by grace and shaped by discipline. God still calls his people to live holy lives, not to distance them from joy, but to draw them into fellowship. When purity precedes progress, presence follows. The God who purified Israel still walks with a purified church.

REFLECTION

1. Why did God emphasize purity before allowing Israel to march from Sinai?

2. How do the cleansing rituals in Numbers 5 show both God's holiness and his mercy?

3. What can the Nazirite vow teach modern Christians about voluntary devotion?

4. Why is obedience, even in repetitive or routine acts, essential for spiritual unity?

5. In what ways does God's order in Numbers 5–10 challenge our tendency toward spiritual chaos?

6. How does God's blessing in Numbers 6 reveal that purity leads to joyful communion?

DISCUSSION

1. What does "God's presence requires purity" look like in a congregation's daily life?

2. How can Christians pursue holiness without drifting into legalism or self-righteousness?

3. In what ways does church discipline or accountability reflect the principle of a "pure camp"?

4. Why do you think God valued repetition and uniformity in the tribes' offerings?

5. What might it look like for the church to "move with the cloud" today?

6. How can the principles of Numbers 5–10 help us prepare for God's mission in our world?

3

COMPLAINTS & QUAIL

NUMBERS 10:11–11:35

Objective: To emphasize that discontent rejects God's goodness and destroys trust in his faithful provision.

INTRODUCTION

A man once joked that no matter how good life gets, people still find something to gripe about. "If I ever win the lottery," he said, "I'll probably complain about the taxes." His humor hides a painful truth: human beings have a knack for turning blessings into burdens. Gratitude fades faster than manna melts in the sun. Israel proved this only three days into their journey from Sinai.

After a year of preparation, purification, and organization, the nation finally set out toward the Promised Land. Trumpets sounded, the cloud lifted, and hope filled the air. But soon, the music of obedience gave way to the murmur of complaint. The people grumbled about hardship, then about food, longing for Egypt's menu instead of God's mercy. Their cravings were more than culinary—they were spiritual rebellion. Discontent didn't simply express discomfort; it denied God's goodness.

Numbers 10:11–11:35 reminds us that complaining is not a minor flaw but a major sin. It questions God's wisdom, timing, and care. The fire at Taberah and the graves at Kibroth-hattaavah stand as warning markers on the road from grace to grumbling. Yet amid judgment, God's mercy still shines. He provided quail for the hungry and Spirit for the weary. Contentment is an act of faith, and complaint is rebellion disguised as realism.

EXAMINATION

From Sinai to complaint (10:11–11:3)

After nearly a year camped at Mount Sinai, Israel finally broke camp on "the twentieth day of the second month" (10:11). The cloud lifted from the tabernacle, signaling that it was time to move. Trumpets sounded, tribes fell into formation, and the wilderness of Sinai stretched before them. Everything about the opening verses suggests anticipation and order. God's people, purified and prepared, were finally on the march toward promise.

But the excitement didn't last. In a jarring transition, the narrative pivots from movement to mutiny: "And the people complained in the hearing of the Lord about their misfortunes" (11:1). The Hebrew implies habitual grumbling—constant murmuring that erodes gratitude. Though they had seen Sinai's fire, eaten manna, and heard God's voice, their hearts still longed for comfort more than communion. The text says God's anger was kindled, and fire consumed part of the outskirts of the camp. The place was named *Taberah* ("burning"), a warning that ingratitude scorches fellowship.

This moment sets the tone for the rest of Numbers. The people had left Sinai physically, but spiritually they were still in Egypt. Complaining, not unbelief alone, became the dominant expression of rebellion. It is no coincidence that this first rebellion occurred right after Israel's formal organization. Structure without faith only magnifies frustration. They were prepared for movement but not for trust.

Israel's grumbling was not about discomfort but about sovereignty—they questioned whether God's way was good. The same temptation still haunts Christians: when obedience leads through barren places, we assume something must be wrong with God's plan. The fire at Taberah reminds us that complaint is not a small sin—it's a refusal to trust God's goodness.

Craving and contempt (11:4–9)

The first complaint faded, but soon another began—this time about food. The "rabble" among them (likely non-Israelites who had joined the exodus) begin craving the delicacies of Egypt: fish, cucumbers, melons, leeks, onions, and garlic. Their nostalgia became contagious, and the Israelites joined in: "Who will give us meat to eat?" (11:4). Memory became selective; slavery was forgotten. They despised the manna God provided.

This passage exposes the anatomy of discontent. First comes *dissatisfaction*—an ache for more than what God gives. Then *distortion*—the false belief that life was better without him. Finally comes *disdain*—open contempt for his provision. Sin begins with appetite and ends with accusation. What started as hunger becomes rebellion.

The text goes out of its way to describe manna as a daily miracle. It looked like coriander seed, tasted like cakes baked with oil, and fell each morning with the dew. It required gathering and grinding but never failed. Yet the people's contempt for manna was contempt for God himself. Their complaint was theological: "We loathe this worthless food" (21:5). In their eyes, God's provision was bland and boring—proof that hearts fed by grace can still crave Egypt's spice cabinet.

The craving for meat was less about diet and more about desire for independence. To want meat in the desert was to say, "We don't trust God to sustain us." The people's appetite exposed unbelief disguised as nostalgia. Their stomachs remembered Egypt fondly, but their souls had forgotten the chains.

Moses' burden and God's provision (11:10–30)

Even Moses began to feel the weight of the people's discontent. Their weeping echoed through the camp, and the great leader broke down before God: "Why have you dealt ill with your servant? ... I am not able to carry all this people alone; the burden is too heavy for me" (11:11, 14). The Hebrew term for "burden" recalls Exodus 18, where Jethro warned Moses about exhaustion. Here, however, the weight was not administrative—it was emotional. Moses felt crushed by complaint.

His outburst bordered on despair. "If you will treat me like this, kill me at once" (11:15). The man who faced Pharaoh now pled for relief from his own people. Yet even here, God responded with compassion. He instructed Moses to gather seventy elders, upon whom he would place a portion of the Spirit resting on Moses. This moment became a divine delegation: the burden of leadership was distributed and shared. God met frustration with fellowship. The Spirit who empowered Moses now filled others to help sustain the community. Leadership fatigue is real, but God's provision is greater.

Alongside this spiritual remedy, God promised a physical one: "You shall eat meat … not one day, or two days, or five days … but a whole month, until it comes out at your nostrils" (11:19–20). The tone is both ironic and severe. God would grant their craving, but in abundance that exposed their folly. They would taste the consequences of discontent.

Judgment and mercy (11:31–35)

The final scene at Kibroth-hattaavah ("graves of craving") completes the story. A wind from the Lord brought quail from the sea, covering the camp for miles in every direction. The people gathered greedily—no less than ten homers each, enough to feed families for weeks. Their craving overwhelmed caution. But "while the meat was still between their teeth, before it was consumed, the anger of the Lord was kindled against the people, and the Lord struck down the people with a very great plague" (11:33). The place of indulgence became a cemetery of appetite.

The tragedy lies not only in their death but in their blindness. They saw God's glory in Sinai's fire and tasted his grace in daily bread, yet they demanded more. The people's craving for meat was the final refusal of grace—they no longer believed that what God provided was good. Discontent had matured into rebellion.

Yet even in judgment, mercy lingered. The camp moved on. God continued to guide them by cloud and fire. Moses still interceded, the Spirit still rested on the elders, and manna still fell. God disciplined his people, but he did not abandon them. His patience proved as persistent as their complaining.

Numbers 11 stands as one of Scripture's clearest warnings against grumbling. Discontent is not a mild flaw; it's a declaration of war against divine goodness. The chapter's progression—complaint, craving, contempt, and catastrophe—shows how unbelief grows when gratitude fades. It's no coincidence that Paul warned the Corinthians not to "grumble as some of them did" (1 Cor. 10:10). The wilderness generation becomes a mirror for every Christian who doubts that God's way is best.

The story of the quail is about the danger of despising grace. When we demand what God withholds, we lose joy in what he gives. Israel's rebellion reminds us that divine discipline is not cruelty but mercy's last resort.

God's fire at Taberah, his Spirit at the tent, and his plague at Kibroth-hattaavah all declare that the goodness of God must be trusted, not tested.

APPLICATION

1. Discontent distorts our memory of grace

Israel's longing for Egypt shows how easily gratitude can fade. They remembered fish and garlic but forgot the chains. When life grows difficult, the past always seems sweeter than it was. Discontent doesn't just complain about the present—it rewrites history. Christians are not immune. We idealize "simpler times," envy others' blessings, or imagine life was easier before obedience demanded sacrifice. Yet every backward glance risks minimizing the slavery of sin. God's people are called to remember redemption, not nostalgia. Gratitude guards against distortion. When we rehearse what God has done—our forgiveness, his faithfulness, his patience—the cravings for "Egypt" lose power. The cure for complaint is memory sanctified by grace. We must remind ourselves that what God rescues us from is never better than what he leads us to.

2. Grumbling is rebellion in disguise

Complaint feels harmless, but in Numbers 11 it became open revolt. The people weren't just hungry; they were accusing God of failure. Discontent questions his wisdom, timing, and care. Every "why me?" whispered in frustration risks echoing Israel's rebellion. Scripture repeatedly warns that grumbling corrodes faith from within. Paul wrote that Israel's wilderness failures were recorded "as examples for us" (1 Cor. 10:6). When we murmur against leadership, circumstances, or one another, we are not venting frustration—we are challenging divine goodness. Gratitude, by contrast, is an act of submission. It acknowledges that God knows what he's doing even when we don't. The lesson from Kibroth-hattaavah is sobering: discontentment may begin with appetite, but it ends in accusation. The heart that cannot trust God's provision will soon resist his purpose.

3. God's provision tests our trust

The manna that fell daily was more than sustenance—it was a test. Each morning Israel had to trust that God would provide tomorrow's portion.

But faith grew weary of routine. They wanted variety, not dependence. Likewise, Christians often crave change when God calls for contentment. We want the dramatic while he offers the daily. The question is not whether God provides, but whether we trust him to provide in his way and time. His mercies are new every morning, yet we grumble that they look the same. When we stop seeing God's gifts as miracles, we start seeing them as monotonous. Spiritual maturity means receiving ordinary grace with extraordinary gratitude. The same God who fed Israel in the desert feeds our souls today through his Word and presence—if only we learn to be satisfied with him.

4. Leadership requires shared burdens and divine dependence

Moses' collapse under the weight of complaint reminds us that even the strongest leaders cannot carry God's people alone. The seventy elders were not a concession to weakness but an affirmation of divine order. In times of discontent, leaders need partners who share both the work and the wounds. Churches that expect one person to bear every load soon reproduce Moses' exhaustion. But when Spirit-filled servants rise to help, burdens turn to blessings. Moses' cry, "I am not able to carry this people alone," becomes a model of humble dependence. Leadership that leans on God and invites others to serve creates a healthier, holier community. Grumbling isolates; shared service unites. The Spirit who empowered seventy elders still strengthens the weary today.

CONCLUSION

Israel's journey from Sinai began with order but descended into outrage. Their complaints revealed not hunger but unbelief—a refusal to trust the goodness of God. In his mercy, God still fed and led them, but he also disciplined them so they would learn that grumbling and gratitude cannot share the same heart. Numbers 11 stands as a warning for all who think they deserve more than grace. Discontent always whispers that God is holding out on us; faith insists that he has given us everything we need. The wilderness teaches that contentment is not found in changing circumstances but in trusting the unchanging goodness of God.

REFLECTION

1. Why does complaint against God's plan reveal a lack of trust in his goodness?
2. How did Israel's craving for Egypt's food distort their memory of life in bondage?
3. What ordinary gifts of God do you tend to overlook or take for granted?
4. How does gratitude act as a safeguard against discontent and rebellion?
5. In what ways can leadership fatigue develop when people grumble instead of serve?
6. How does this story show that God's discipline is both severe and merciful?

DISCUSSION

1. What forms of discontent most often tempt believers or congregations today?
2. How can Christians cultivate contentment in a culture built on constant dissatisfaction?
3. When does healthy lament cross the line into sinful complaint?
4. What practical steps can a church take to share leadership burdens more effectively?
5. How should we respond when God gives us what we asked for—but it exposes our sin?
6. What does Numbers 11 teach about trusting God's provision even when it feels monotonous?

4

REBELLION IN THE CAMP

NUMBERS 12–14

Objective: To show that unbelief lies at the heart of rebellion and robs God's people of blessing.

INTRODUCTION

A young boy stood on the edge of a swimming pool, shivering with fear. His father waited in the water below, arms open, saying, "Jump—I'll catch you." The boy wanted to believe him, but the water looked deep and cold. He hesitated, inching backward. Finally, the father said gently, "If you can't trust me here, how will you ever learn to swim?" Trust required a leap.

Israel stood at a similar edge. After months of preparation and countless demonstrations of God's power, they arrived at the border of the Promised Land. All they had to do was trust the One who had brought them this far. But when the moment came to jump, unbelief froze them in place. They could sing about God's faithfulness at Sinai, but they couldn't stake their future on it at Kadesh-barnea.

Numbers 12–14 tells the story of a people paralyzed by doubt. Miriam and Aaron rebelled against Moses' leadership, ten spies spread fear, and the nation refused to move forward. At every turn, unbelief disguised itself as caution, complaint, or pride. The result was a generation sentenced to wander. Their story teaches that rebellion doesn't begin with disobedience—it begins with distrust. Faith is not merely agreeing that God is powerful; it's stepping into the deep because we believe he is good.

EXAMINATION

Family rebellion (12:1–16)

In this chapter, rebellion comes not from the rabble at the camp's edge but from Moses' own family. Miriam and Aaron spoke against him "because of the Cushite woman whom he had married" (12:1). Their complaint about marriage masked a deeper issue: envy. "Has the Lord indeed spoken only through Moses? Has he not spoken through us also?" (12:2). What looks like family tension was really spiritual insubordination. Pride is unbelief wearing religious clothes.

The Lord's response was immediate and severe. He summoned the three siblings to the tent of meeting, descending in the pillar of cloud to settle the matter himself. God distinguished between Moses and every other prophet. Others received visions or dreams, but Moses spoke with God "mouth to mouth" (12:8). The text is clear: proximity to God is not a platform for pride but a test of humility.

Then judgment fell. Miriam, apparently the ringleader, became leprous—her skin white as snow. Ironically, the one who complained about her brother's foreign wife now bore the mark of uncleanness. Aaron pleaded for mercy, and Moses, in contrast to his critics, interceded for his sister: "O God, please heal her—please." God's answer was firm but compassionate: Miriam must bear her shame for seven days outside the camp, then be restored.

This episode reveals the seedbed of all rebellion—unbelief in God's appointed order. Miriam and Aaron doubted that God knew what he was doing in choosing Moses. Pride questions God's wisdom; unbelief resists his will. Even the most intimate relationships can fracture when faith gives way to ambition.

The spies sent (13:1–24)

After family rebellion came national testing. God instructed Moses to send twelve spies—one from each tribe—to explore Canaan. The mission itself was not sinful; it was a normal reconnaissance before conquest. The problem would arise not in what they saw, but in how they interpreted it.

The spies traveled from the southern wilderness to the northern reaches of Hamath, surveying a land as diverse as it was fertile. They cut a cluster of grapes so large it took two men to carry it on a pole—a vivid symbol of abundance. God's promise was not exaggerated. Everything about the report should have inspired confidence. The land truly flowed with milk and honey.

Yet even before they returned, the narrative hints at tension. The mention of the Anakim—giants associated with fortified cities—prepares the reader for the crisis ahead. The spies' journey was not simply about geography; it was about faith. The spies' mission was a mirror of Israel's heart—would they see the land through the lens of promise or peril? God allowed this test to expose their unbelief.

The report and the rebellion (13:25–14:12)

After forty days, the spies returned. Their initial report confirmed the land's goodness but quickly turned to fear: "However, the people who dwell in the land are strong, and the cities are fortified and very large" (13:28). The conjunction "however" marks the turning point from faith to fear. Ten of the twelve spies focused on obstacles rather than opportunity. They magnified giants and minimized God.

Caleb's voice broke through the panic: "Let us go up at once and occupy it, for we are well able to overcome it" (13:30). He saw with the eyes of faith, not sight. But the other spies spread a "bad report," exaggerating dangers and undermining morale. "We seemed to ourselves like grasshoppers," they say (13:33). Their fear became contagious, and by chapter 14, the entire congregation wept through the night.

What follows is one of Scripture's darkest scenes of collective unbelief. The people accused God of cruelty: "Would that we had died in Egypt!" (14:2). They proposed appointing a new leader to take them back to bondage. Unbelief always rewrites history—it makes Egypt look like salvation and obedience like suicide.

Moses and Aaron fell facedown, pleading for the people to stop. Joshua and Caleb tore their clothes, urging the crowd to trust God's promise: "The Lord is with us; do not fear them" (14:9). But the mob's response was chilling—they picked up stones to kill them. When unbelief matures, it doesn't just resist God's word; it silences those who speak it. The glory of the Lord appeared at the tent of meeting, halting the rebellion before blood is shed. God's patience has limits. The same God who had pardoned grumbling now confronted full-fledged mutiny.

Moses' intercession and God's judgment (14:13-38)

God declared his intention to destroy the nation and start over with Moses. Yet Moses interceded again, not appealing to Israel's worthiness but to God's reputation: "The Egyptians will hear of it … they will say, 'Because the Lord was not able to bring this people into the land, he has killed them in the wilderness'" (14:13-16). Moses pleaded for God's mercy to uphold God's name. This prayer is one of the most moving intercessions in the Bible.

Moses reminded God of his own self-revelation: "The Lord is slow to anger and abounding in steadfast love" (14:18; see Exod. 34:6). His argument was theological—God must act consistently with his character. The Lord agreed to pardon, but the pardon did not erase consequences. The unbelieving generation would wander forty years—one year for each day the spies scouted the land—until every adult who despised the promise died. Only Joshua and Caleb, who "had a different spirit," would enter Canaan.

Here, unbelief reached its natural end: exclusion from blessing. God's presence remained with Israel, but his promise waited for a generation that would trust him. The same desert that once tested faith now became its graveyard. Unbelief is not merely doubt—it is active defiance against the reliability of God's word. Israel's refusal to enter the land replayed Eden's original sin: distrusting the goodness of what God gives.

The false repentance (14:39-45)

The next morning, remorse replaced rebellion—but it was the wrong kind. The people mourned their fate and resolved to enter the land anyway. "We have sinned," they said, "but we will go up to the place that the Lord has promised" (14:40). Their confession sounds sincere, but it was motivated by regret, not repentance. Moses warned them that God's presence would not go with them, but they went anyway. Unbelief refuses to listen even when it sounds religious.

The result was predictable and tragic. The Amalekites and Canaanites descended and routed them. Their zeal without faith led to defeat. They experienced in miniature what unbelief always produces—loss without learning. The same people who refused to fight with God's help now tried to fight without him. Their story ended not in triumph but in retreat.

This passage offers a sobering portrait of counterfeit repentance. Sorrow alone cannot undo rebellion. True faith submits to God's timing, not merely his promises. Israel wanted Canaan on their terms, not his. Unbelief always insists on control—it would rather die trying than live trusting.

From Miriam's jealousy to the spies' fear and the people's false repentance, Numbers 12–14 exposes unbelief as the root of every rebellion. Pride, fear, and stubbornness all grow from the same soil: a refusal to trust God's goodness. The result is paralysis, punishment, and prolonged wandering. But even here, grace remains. God continued to dwell among his people, providing manna, guidance, and hope for a new generation. His patience, though tested, outlasted their failure.

Israel's tragedy becomes our warning. The writer of Hebrews echoes it centuries later: "Take care, brothers, lest there be in any of you an evil, unbelieving heart, leading you to fall away from the living God" (Heb. 3:12). The antidote to rebellion is faith—faith that God's commands are good, his promises reliable, and his presence worth every risk.

APPLICATION

1. Unbelief begins where trust ends

The story of Israel's rebellion teaches that unbelief is not ignorance but rejection. The people had seen God's power in Egypt, heard his voice at Sinai, and eaten his manna daily. Their problem wasn't lack of evidence—it was lack of trust. Faith fades when the heart no longer believes that God is good. The spies' fear and the people's tears exposed a deeper disease: they trusted their perception more than God's promise. The same temptation stalks Christians today. We doubt God's timing, question his plan, and redefine obedience to suit our comfort. Unbelief rarely announces itself; it grows quietly in our complaints and our caution. Trust in God's character, not our circumstances, is the only cure. Faith doesn't ignore obstacles—it remembers who walks before us.

2. Pride is unbelief in disguise

Miriam and Aaron's criticism of Moses shows how easily unbelief hides behind pride. They envied Moses' influence but cloaked it in spiritual language. When pride whispers, "I could do it better," it's not ambition—it's unbelief that God knows best. Every challenge to divinely ordered leadership stems from distrust in God's wisdom. The church today faces the same danger. When members resist elders' guidance or belittle others' roles, they mimic Miriam's envy. God's judgment of her leprosy is a stark reminder that rebellion often wears the mask of righteousness. True humility believes that God's structure for his people—whether in family, church, or ministry—is wise and good. Faith rests in his appointments; pride questions them. Where trust thrives, submission becomes joy, not humiliation.

3. Fear magnifies giants and minimizes God

The spies saw the same land, the same cities, and the same giants—but not the same God. Ten saw danger; two saw promise. Unbelief distorts reality. It shrinks God to the size of our fears and inflates our obstacles beyond measure. Fearful faith is not faith at all; it's self-preservation disguised as prudence. When we focus on the "giants," we forget the God who topples them. Caleb's courage came not from optimism but from theology: "The Lord is with us; do not fear them." Faith always interprets circumstances through God's power, not the other way around. Christians today face intimidating challenges—cultural pressure, moral decay, personal weakness—but the same truth applies. The God who parted the sea still keeps his promises. Fear is not humility; it's unbelief forgetting who God is.

4. False repentance leads to ruin

When Israel tried to enter Canaan after God had forbidden it, they mistook regret for repentance. They mourned consequences but not sin. True repentance submits to God's word, even when it delays blessing. False repentance insists on control—it wants forgiveness without surrender. The church often repeats this mistake when we rush to fix disobedience by our own efforts instead of bowing before God's authority. Spiritual enthusiasm cannot replace spiritual obedience. Israel's defeat at Hormah proves that zeal without faith is self-destruction. God's timing is part of God's promise; to reject one is to lose both. Real repentance accepts correction, trusts divine wisdom, and waits for God's leading. Faith doesn't run ahead—it walks in step with grace.

CONCLUSION

Israel's rebellion at Kadesh was not born from ignorance but from unbelief. They knew God's promises yet doubted his goodness. Fear replaced faith, and hesitation became disobedience. The result was forty years of wandering—a whole generation lost to doubt. Numbers 12–14 warns that rebellion often begins in the heart long before it reaches the hands. Pride, jealousy, and fear all grow from the same root: a failure to trust that God's way is best. Yet even in judgment, God's mercy endures. He remains faithful to his covenant and raises up a new generation to believe. The choice remains the same for us—faith that moves forward, or unbelief that dies standing still.

REFLECTION

1. Why does Numbers 12–14 portray unbelief as the true source of rebellion?

2. How did Miriam and Aaron's jealousy reveal a lack of trust in God's choices?

3. What causes people today to focus on "giants" rather than God's promises?

4. How does fear reshape our view of God's character and power?

5. Why is regret different from repentance, and how can we tell the difference?

6. What does this passage teach about God's patience in the face of repeated unbelief?

DISCUSSION

1. How can churches guard against unbelief that hides beneath pride or complaint?

2. What habits help strengthen trust in God when circumstances seem overwhelming?

3. In what ways do we still "test" God's goodness as Israel did?

4. What are some modern examples of false repentance—sorrow without surrender?

5. How can spiritual leaders today share burdens as Moses did without losing faith?

6. How does this story help Christians understand the seriousness of distrusting God's word?

5

TESTS OF AUTHORITY
NUMBERS 15-17

Objective: To warn that resisting God-ordained leadership brings judgment, while humble submission preserves life and unity.

INTRODUCTION

Authority is easy to resent when you're not the one holding it. In a fire station, a rookie once complained that his captain barked too many orders and demanded too much precision. One day, the captain let him lead a drill. When the alarm rang, confusion erupted—hoses tangled, commands overlapped, and seconds slipped away. The rookie realized that authority isn't arrogance; it's order that saves lives. Leadership, rightly exercised, protects everyone under it.

Israel struggled to learn that lesson. In Numbers 15-17, the nation faced repeated tests of authority. After the catastrophe at Kadesh, the people still questioned whether Moses and Aaron had any right to lead them. Some defied God's commands outright, others disguised rebellion as reform. Korah and his followers claimed equality but sought power. Their challenge was not about fairness; it was about rejecting the structure God had set in place.

These chapters remind us that rebellion against God's appointed leadership is rebellion against God himself. The Sabbath breaker, the jealous

Levite, and the murmuring crowd all discovered that divine order is not negotiable. Yet even amid judgment, God affirmed his mercy—Aaron's budding rod showed that life flourishes where submission replaces pride. Numbers 15-17 teaches that true authority is sacred, and challenging it invites ruin. God's people find peace only when they honor his design.

EXAMINATION

Grace after rebellion (15:1-31)

After the devastating judgment at Kadesh-barnea, when Israel's unbelief condemned an entire generation to wander, the narrative takes an unexpected turn. God spoke again—not in wrath, but in reassurance (15:2). Despite their failure, God's promise still stood. The chapter's first words restored hope: he had not abandoned them.

This section outlines laws about grain, oil, and drink offerings. Though seemingly routine, these commands were profoundly gracious. They assumed that Israel would reach Canaan. God grounded his authority in mercy. His faithfulness did not cancel his holiness, and his holiness did not cancel his promise. But the instructions also emphasized that obedience had to accompany faith. The offerings signified acknowledgment that God alone sustained life.

Later in the chapter, provision is made for unintentional sins (15:22-29), showing that ignorance required atonement just as willful defiance did. Then, in sharp contrast, the law addressed "high-handed" sin—intentional rebellion (15:30-31). The person who sinned with a raised fist, defiantly rejecting God's rule. Such a person was cut off from the community. This distinction sets the stage for the chapters that followed: grace for weakness, but judgment for rebellion. Israel had to learn that mercy did not soften God's authority; it strengthened it.

The Sabbath breaker and the tassels (15:32-41)

To illustrate deliberate defiance, the narrative inserts a short but striking episode. A man was found gathering sticks on the Sabbath. The people detained him until the Lord revealed the penalty: death by stoning. Modern readers flinch, but the story underscores that rebellion is not measured by the size of the act but by the spirit behind it. Gathering sticks on the

Sabbath symbolized contempt for God's command—a public statement that his word could be ignored.

This execution shocked Israel into attention. God immediately followed with a reminder meant to prevent future rebellion. He commanded that every Israelite attach tassels with blue cords to the corners of their garments (15:38–40). Each thread served as a visual sermon—"remember all the commandments of the Lord, to do them." The color blue, associated with the sky and the tabernacle, reminded them that heaven governed their lives.

This sequence—sin, judgment, symbol—reveals divine pedagogy. God instructed his people through consequence and reminder. The tassels turned obedience into something visible and habitual, embedding faithfulness into daily life. But they also anticipated the deeper truth fulfilled in Christ: God would one day write his law not on garments but on hearts (Jer. 31:33). Until then, Israel had to learn that holiness required more than ritual—it demanded reverence for divine authority.

Korah's revolt (16:1–40)

The most dramatic challenge to God's leadership followed. Korah, a Levite from the clan of Kohath, gathered 250 community leaders and confronted Moses and Aaron. Their accusation sounded democratic: "You have gone too far! For all in the congregation are holy, every one of them, and the Lord is among them. Why then do you exalt yourselves above the assembly of the Lord?" (16:3). On the surface, it was a call for equality. In reality, it was a revolt against God's structure.

Korah's complaint distorted truth with pious language. Yes, the congregation was holy—but by God's appointment, not by self-assertion. Korah's rebellion revealed the heart of all insubordination: the desire for status without submission. His followers, drawn from Reuben's tribe and Israel's elders, represented both priestly ambition and political opportunism. The entire community faced a leadership crisis disguised as reform.

Moses' response was instructive. He fell facedown, a posture of humility rather than defensiveness. He proposed a test: the rebels would bring censers with incense before the Lord, and God would show whom he had chosen. The next day, each man stood at the tabernacle entrance with a censer. The scene brims with tension—holy fire in the hands of unholy men.

God's judgment was swift. The earth opened and swallowed Korah, Dathan, and Abiram, along with their families and possessions. Fire consumed the 250 leaders offering unauthorized incense. The censers were then hammered into plates to overlay the altar, serving as a permanent reminder that only those whom God appointed could serve before him. The rebellion meant to democratize holiness ended in devastation. God's message was unmistakable: rejecting divinely established authority was not bravery—it was blasphemy.

Intercession and plague (16:41–50)

Amazingly, the very next day, the entire congregation turned against Moses and Aaron again, accusing them: "You have killed the people of the Lord!" (16:41). The irony was staggering. They witnessed divine judgment and blamed the mediators. Human hearts often responded to correction with resentment rather than repentance. As the crowd assembled, the cloud covered the tabernacle, and God's glory appeared. A plague broke out, spreading rapidly through the camp.

Moses reacted instantly: "Take your censer, and put fire on it from off the altar ... and make atonement for them, for wrath has gone out from the Lord; the plague has begun" (16:46). Aaron ran with the censer into the midst of the people, standing between the dead and the living. The plague stopped. Nearly 15,000 died, but countless others were saved because one man interceded.

This episode contrasted two kinds of leadership. Korah's followers used incense to promote themselves; Aaron used it to preserve others. The difference was motive—selfish ambition versus sacrificial service. True authority stood in the gap, not on a pedestal. God validates leaders who serve through obedience, not those who grasp for power.

The censers that brought death now became instruments of memory. Leadership, once contested, was reaffirmed through mercy. God's wrath revealed his justice; Aaron's mediation revealed his grace. Together they showed that spiritual authority exists not to dominate but to deliver.

Aaron's rod that budded (17:1–13)

To silence the unrest once and for all, God provided a final sign. Each tribe's leader was to bring a staff—a symbol of authority—and place it before the ark. The staff belonging to the man God chose would blossom. Twelve rods were laid before the Lord overnight. In the morning, Aaron's rod, representing the tribe of Levi, had sprouted, blossomed, and produced ripe almonds. Life sprang from lifeless wood.

The miracle was not arbitrary. Almond trees were among the first to bloom after winter, symbolizing vigilance and new life. God's choice of Aaron's rod confirmed his watchfulness over Israel's worship. Leadership belonged not to those who demanded it, but to those whom God animated with his life-giving power. The dead wood of human ambition could never produce spiritual fruit.

When the people saw the miracle, terror replaced rebellion. "Behold, we perish, we are undone!" they cried (17:12). Their fear, though extreme, signaled understanding at last. They grasped that approaching God on their own terms led only to death. Aaron's budding rod was kept as a testimony before the ark—proof that life flowed through submission, not defiance.

This final act completed the cycle begun with Korah's rebellion. God vindicated his chosen servants and reasserted that holiness was not a human achievement but a divine appointment. The same God who opened the earth now opened a branch. Judgment and grace met in the same hand.

Through these chapters, Israel learned that rebellion is rarely about policy or personality—it is about pride. Korah's camp mistook equality for entitlement, forgetting that God's authority is always benevolent. Leaders are not self-made but God-called, and when people reject them, they reject the One who sent them.

Yet the lessons are also hopeful. God's authority, though unyielding, is life-giving. The earth swallowed rebels, but the rod blossomed for the faithful. Authority abused destroys, but authority submitted to brings flourishing. The danger of challenging God-ordained leadership is not simply institutional chaos—it is spiritual death. To resist God's structure is to resist his presence; to honor it is to find peace under his rule.

APPLICATION

1. Rebellion against leadership is rebellion against God

Korah's revolt was not simply a mutiny against Moses and Aaron; it was a rejection of God's authority. The rebels wrapped their insubordination in spiritual language—"All the congregation is holy"—but their real issue was pride. They wanted position without permission, honor without obedience. The same danger lingers today. When Christians resist the guidance of faithful leaders, undermine godly elders, or disregard Scripture's authority, they echo Korah's cry. God takes rebellion personally because it challenges his wisdom in appointing leaders for his people's good. The earth may not open beneath our feet, but spiritual collapse still follows when we defy divine order. Healthy churches thrive where members respect leadership as God's design, not man's invention.

2. True authority serves rather than seizes

Korah grasped for leadership; Aaron interceded for life. The contrast is stark. One used incense to glorify himself; the other used it to save others. God validates authority marked by humility and sacrifice, not ambition. Jesus echoed this truth when he said, "Whoever would be great among you must be your servant" (Matt. 20:26). In God's kingdom, greatness is measured by service. Spiritual leaders must remember that their authority is derivative—borrowed, not owned. They are stewards, not sovereigns. Likewise, those who follow must see that godly authority exists for their benefit. When leaders lay down their lives for the flock, they mirror Christ, our ultimate High Priest. Rebellion thrives when leadership becomes self-serving, but it dies where authority kneels to serve.

3. Obedience protects community from destruction

Each act of defiance in Numbers 15–17 brought death to the camp. The Sabbath breaker, Korah's rebels, and the grumbling crowd all illustrate that disobedience endangers everyone. Sin is never private—it spreads like contagion. The same is true in the church. When we challenge God's commands or disregard his boundaries, others are drawn into the fallout. Yet obedience, like Aaron's intercession, can stand "between the dead and the living." Our faithfulness has a preserving effect. Families, congregations, and communities are stabilized when God's people honor his Word. Obedience is not drudgery—it is protection. The tassels on Israel's garments served as constant reminders that holiness safeguards life. When Christians walk in submission to God's authority, they become instruments of peace rather than agents of chaos.

4. God vindicates the faithful in his time

Aaron did not defend himself when accused. He waited, and God caused his lifeless rod to bloom. The same God still vindicates those who serve quietly and trust him to reveal the truth. In life, accusations will come. Some will challenge your motives or question your calling. Defending yourself may only deepen division, but trusting God invites vindication rooted in grace. The budding rod teaches that divine affirmation often follows divine testing. Blossoms come after the storm. When leaders remain faithful through criticism, God brings forth fruit that proves his blessing. The One who caused dead wood to flower can bring beauty out of endurance. Faith waits for God to make clear what only he can confirm.

CONCLUSION

Israel's repeated defiance in Numbers 15–17 reveals that rebellion against leadership is rebellion against the Lord who appoints it. The Sabbath breaker defied God's word, Korah defied God's structure, and the congregation defied God's justice. Yet through every judgment, God reaffirmed his mercy. Aaron's intercession stopped the plague, and his budding rod restored peace to a restless nation. Divine authority exists not to suppress but to sustain. When God's people submit to his order, life blossoms; when they resist it, destruction follows. The same truth governs the church today—peace and fruitfulness flourish where God's leadership is honored and his authority obeyed.

REFLECTION

1. Why does rebellion against spiritual leadership ultimately reflect rebellion against God himself?

2. How do the stories of the Sabbath breaker and Korah reveal different forms of defiance?

3. What does Aaron's intercession teach us about the heart of true leadership?

4. Why is obedience a safeguard rather than a restriction in the life of God's people?

5. In what ways does God's vindication of Aaron's rod encourage patience?

6. How can we recognize pride when it disguises itself as zeal for fairness or equality?

DISCUSSION

1. How should believers respond when they disagree with spiritual leaders?

2. What safeguards can churches create to ensure leadership remains humble and accountable?

3. Why do people today still find submission to authority uncomfortable or threatening?

4. What are the dangers of confusing human ambition with divine calling?

5. How can Aaron's example shape the way we pray for and support our leaders?

6. What lessons from Numbers 15–17 apply to maintaining unity in the church today?

6

SIN, WATER, & LEADERSHIP

NUMBERS 18–20

Objective: To show that God's faithfulness endures even when his leaders falter or fail.

INTRODUCTION

A relay race depends on the clean passing of a baton. The fastest runner can lose everything if the handoff fumbles. In those tense seconds, success hinges on precision, trust, and continuity. The team's goal is not individual glory but finishing together. Israel's journey through the wilderness worked much the same way. Each generation—and each leader—was handed responsibility for guiding God's people toward his promise. But unlike a human race, this relay had a perfect Coach who never failed, even when his runners stumbled.

Numbers 18–20 captures this tension between human weakness and divine faithfulness. Aaron and his sons are reminded of their sacred duties, symbolizing God's ongoing presence among a flawed people. A red heifer provides cleansing from death's contamination—proof that holiness still has a pathway even in a defiled world. Then, at Meribah, Moses' temper fractures his ministry, and Aaron dies atop Mount Hor. Leadership falters; mortality intrudes. Yet through it all, God remains constant. Water still flows from the rock, purification still comes through sacrifice, and the priesthood continues through Eleazar.

This section reminds Christians that the reliability of God's promise never depends on the reliability of his servants. Leaders may fall short, but God's grace never does. His faithfulness holds the baton firmly until the race is won.

EXAMINATION

Responsibilities of the priesthood (18:1–32)

After Korah's rebellion, Israel needed reassurance that God's covenant order still stood. The community had just witnessed devastating judgment, and questions surely lingered: Who might draw near? How could sinners live before a holy God? In response, Numbers 18 opens not with wrath, but with renewal. God spoke again to Aaron, reaffirming both privilege and responsibility. "You and your sons and your father's house with you shall bear the iniquity connected with the sanctuary" (18:1). In other words, leadership in sacred things is not a platform for pride—it is a burden of accountability.

The priests were reminded that their ministry was protective. They were to guard both the sanctuary and the altar "that there may never again be wrath on the people of Israel" (18:5). Their work shielded the nation from judgment. God's faithfulness endured through structure; he channeled his holiness through appointed mediators so his presence would not consume the people. The Levites assisted them in daily duties but were not to approach the altar itself. Boundaries were blessings. God's order preserved life, just as fences protected from cliffs.

Then came detailed instructions about provision. The priests would receive the "holy contributions" from Israel—offerings, firstfruits, and tithes. These gifts ensured that the ministers of the tabernacle could serve without distraction. Yet the Levites, unlike the other tribes, were given no land inheritance. Their sustenance was God himself: "I am your portion and your inheritance" (18:20). This arrangement carried deep theological weight. God's faithfulness to the covenant included not just forgiveness but provision for those who kept worship alive. Even in the wilderness, God sustained his servants.

The tithing system also taught that dependence was mutual. Israel depended on priestly intercession, the priests depended on Israel's offerings, and all depended on God's generosity. Divine order produces communal harmony. Leadership, provision, and worship remain intertwined. This renewed arrangement after rebellion demonstrated God's mercy. Despite human failure, he reestablished the relationship. His faithfulness did not end when his people faltered—it rebuilt what rebellion tried to break.

The red heifer and purification (19:1–22)

After reaffirming the priesthood, God turned to the problem of death. Chapter 19 introduces one of Scripture's most mysterious ceremonies—the sacrifice of the red heifer. The ritual seems strange: a perfect red cow, never yoked, was slaughtered and burned outside the camp. Cedarwood, hyssop, and scarlet yarn were thrown into the fire. The ashes were gathered and later mixed with water to create the "water for impurity," used to cleanse those who had touched a corpse.

This procedure addressed a grim reality: death saturated wilderness life. In the desert, graves dotted the landscape. Every funeral threatened to defile those who handled the body. Since God's holiness could not coexist with corruption, he provided a paradoxical remedy—life from ashes, purity through sacrifice. The ashes of the red heifer symbolized God's victory over defilement. Contact with death was inevitable, but separation from God was not.

Every detail communicated theology. The animal's flawless redness suggested completeness of sacrifice; the burning outside the camp paralleled later sin offerings made "outside the gate," a phrase Hebrews used for Christ's crucifixion (Heb. 13:11–12). The addition of cedar and hyssop—materials associated with cleansing lepers (Lev. 14:4)—linked this ritual to restoration and healing. The entire ceremony prefigured Jesus, whose blood cleansed the conscience "from dead works to serve the living God" (Heb. 9:13–14).

For Israel, the ritual ensured communal life could continue. For readers of faith, it revealed that God's faithfulness provided cleansing even in a world defined by death. The priests and people failed repeatedly, but the ashes remained ready—grace kept in reserve. This chapter stands as a quiet bridge between divine justice and divine mercy. Death might touch God's people, but it would never define them.

Moses' failure at Meribah (20:1–13)

The narrative pace quickens. Years passed, and the new generation stood again at Kadesh. Miriam died, and immediately the people complained about water. The cycle of grumbling resumed as if nothing had been learned. They lamented, "Would that we had perished when our brothers perished before the Lord!" (20:3). Their complaint reopened the wounds of the previous generation's unbelief.

Moses and Aaron responded as they always had—falling facedown before the Lord. God instructed Moses to take the staff and "tell the rock before their eyes to yield its water" (20:8). But frustration had been building. The old leader, weary of decades of complaint, lost composure. Standing before the assembly, Moses cried, "Hear now, you rebels: shall we bring water for you out of this rock?" (20:10). Then he struck the rock twice with his staff. Water gushed out, but Moses' tone and action betrayed a subtle yet serious failure.

What went wrong? God had commanded him to speak to the rock, not strike it. The difference might seem small, but it was crucial. Moses shifted focus from God's word to his own power. In anger, he took credit—"shall *we* bring water for you?"—and thus failed to uphold God's holiness before the people. Leadership failure, especially in positions of spiritual trust, distort how others perceive God.

The Lord's response was swift but measured: "Because you did not believe in me, to uphold me as holy in the eyes of the people, you shall not bring this assembly into the land" (20:12). After forty years of faithful service, Moses forfeited his entrance into Canaan. The sentence is heartbreaking, yet it reveals something deeper—God's faithfulness even in discipline. He still provided water for the thirsty, proving that his mercy flowed despite flawed mediators.

This scene marks a significant moment in Numbers. Moses, the man who once interceded for rebels, now became the one needing grace. His failure at Meribah underscores the insufficiency of human leadership. No matter how godly the person, no one can perfectly represent the holiness of God. Yet God remained faithful, supplying what his servant could not. The rock became a symbol of enduring grace—struck once, but never silent. Paul's later reflection in 1 Corinthians 10:4—"that Rock was Christ"—reminds us that living water ultimately flowed from divine faithfulness, not human success.

Edom's refusal and Aaron's death (20:14-29)

Following Meribah, Israel faced rejection from an unexpected source. Moses sent messengers to Edom, appealing to kinship and promising to travel peacefully through their land. He reminded the king of Edom of Israel's hardships in Egypt and God's deliverance, hoping for brotherly compassion. But Edom refused passage and threatened violence if Israel crossed its borders. The route to Canaan lengthened, and the detour through the wilderness resumed.

This denial echoed an ancient rivalry—Jacob and Esau, Israel and Edom. Yet God's faithfulness remained unshaken. Human hostility could not block divine purpose. Israel turned away, demonstrating obedience to God's direction rather than retaliating. Sometimes faithfulness means retreating rather than retaliating. God's plans were delayed, not derailed.

The chapter then moves to Mount Hor, where God announced Aaron's approaching death. His transgression at Meribah mirrored Moses', and the penalty was the same: he would not enter the land. God instructed Moses to ascend the mountain with Aaron and his son Eleazar. There, in a poignant ceremony, Moses removed Aaron's priestly garments and placed them upon Eleazar. The garments—symbols of mediation and holiness—passed to the next generation. Then Aaron died, and the nation mourned for thirty days.

Aaron's death felt like the closing of an era. The brother who had stood beside Moses in Pharaoh's court, who had lifted the censer "between the dead and the living," now lay still. Yet even here, the narrative hums with divine faithfulness. The priesthood did not die; it continued. The garments of service were not buried but transferred. The God who struck leaders for disobedience still sustained his covenant by succession.

This act prefigured the continuity of Christ's eternal priesthood. In Hebrews 7, Jesus was declared the High Priest who "holds his priesthood permanently, because he continues forever." The transfer from Aaron to Eleazar anticipated that one day a priest would arise who would never need replacement.

These three chapters reveal that the faithfulness of God stood taller than the frailty of his servants. The Levites' duties prove that worship continues because God ordains order. The ashes of the red heifer prove that purification continues because God provides cleansing. The water from the rock proves that mercy continues because God provides grace. The priestly garments passed to Eleazar prove that leadership continues because God provides continuity.

Numbers 18–20 is not a story of perfection but of preservation. Even as leaders stumbled and generations died, God remained the constant in a world of collapse. His holiness never softened, yet his mercy never ceased. The failures of Moses and Aaron anticipated the need for a faultless mediator—a leader who would never misrepresent God's glory nor fail his people. That leader was Jesus Christ, the true and better Moses, who was faithful "as a son over God's house" (Heb. 3:6).

In the end, the wilderness narrative taught one lasting truth: human leadership falters, but divine faithfulness endures. The God who guided Israel through rebellion and death still guides his church through weakness and loss.

APPLICATION

1. God's faithfulness outlasts human failure

The deaths of Miriam and Aaron, and Moses' disobedience at Meribah, could have signaled the end of Israel's hope. Yet the water still flowed, the priesthood continued, and the covenant stood. God's plan is never held hostage by human weakness. Leaders come and go; their mistakes may delay blessing, but they cannot destroy it. God's promises are stronger than our failures. This truth steadies the church today. When spiritual leaders fall or disappoint us, our faith must not collapse with them. The foundation of our hope is not human reliability but divine constancy. God remains faithful when we are faithless, and his purposes march on. We grieve the failures of those we follow, but we do not lose confidence in the One they serve.

2. Holiness still matters, even under grace

God's mercy in these chapters does not cancel his standards. He forgives, but he also disciplines. Moses' punishment may appear harsh, yet it reminds us that those closest to God are held to higher accountability. Grace never excuses irreverence. Leaders, teachers, and servants must handle God's Word and work with reverent care, for holiness is the foundation of faithfulness. The church must resist the modern temptation to treat leadership lightly or holiness casually. God's love is not indulgent; it is refining. His faithfulness includes correction that protects his people from greater harm. Mercy and holiness are not enemies—they are partners in God's covenant care. To honor both is to reflect the heart of the God who forgives yet still calls his people higher.

3. Leadership failure cannot stop divine provision

Moses failed, yet water still gushed from the rock. That miracle reveals a crucial truth: God's blessings depend on his character, not our competence.

Israel's thirst was quenched not because of their leaders, but because of their Lord. In the same way, God continues to nourish his church through imperfect vessels. Preachers, elders, and servants all have flaws, but the grace they convey is flawless. This humbles those who lead and comforts those who follow. God's provision never ceases because his mission never falters. When we witness human weakness in spiritual leadership, we must look beyond the messenger to the Master. The rock still flows, even when struck by trembling hands. Our confidence lies not in leaders who perform perfectly but in the God who provides faithfully.

4. Death cannot halt God's work

Aaron's death atop Mount Hor closes one era and begins another. The priesthood's garments pass from father to son, symbolizing God's unbroken commitment to his people. Leaders die, but the Lord remains. His purposes continue from generation to generation. This truth is both sobering and liberating. No servant of God is indispensable, yet every faithful servant contributes to a work that outlives them. The church must not anchor its hope to personalities but to the eternal Priest who never dies. In Jesus, the pattern of Numbers 20 finds its fulfillment: death gives way to continuity, and failure to faithfulness. God's kingdom advances not because of flawless leaders but because of an unfailing Lord. When death removes one servant, grace raises another, ensuring that the mission never ends.

CONCLUSION

Numbers 18–20 reminds us that God's covenant purposes never collapse under the weight of human failure. Priests grow weary, prophets stumble, and even the greatest leaders disappoint, yet the Lord remains faithful to his word. Moses' anger could not stop the water, Aaron's death could not halt the priesthood, and Israel's rebellion could not cancel God's mercy. His faithfulness outlasts every flaw. For the church today, this truth offers both humility and hope: humility, because no leader is indispensable; hope, because no failure is final. God's work continues through imperfect servants, and his grace flows steadily from the Rock that never runs dry.

REFLECTION

1. How do Numbers 18–20 show that God's plans continue even when leaders fail?

2. What do the priestly duties in chapter 18 teach about accountability and privilege in service?

3. Why was the ritual of the red heifer such a powerful symbol of cleansing and hope?

4. What specific attitude or action caused Moses to misrepresent God at Meribah?

5. How does Aaron's death demonstrate both God's justice and his faithfulness?

6. In what ways can believers today trust God's constancy amid leadership failures or transitions?

DISCUSSION

1. Why do you think God still provided water even after Moses disobeyed him?

2. What does the priesthood's dependence on God's provision teach about leadership and humility?

3. How does the red heifer ceremony foreshadow Christ's ultimate sacrifice for sin and death?

4. What lessons from Moses' failure can church leaders learn about representing God faithfully?

5. Why is it important to remember that God's work continues through imperfect people?

6. How can churches help one another stay focused on God's faithfulness when human leaders disappoint?

7

THE BRONZE SERPENT

NUMBERS 21

Objective: To show that faith brings healing when we look to God's provision with trust and gratitude.

INTRODUCTION

In 1854, a cholera epidemic swept through London. Hundreds were dying, and panic spread faster than the disease itself. A physician named John Snow traced the outbreak to a single contaminated water pump. He marked the handle so people would stop drinking from it, and soon the epidemic subsided. Healing began when people trusted the warning and looked to a different source for water. Faith required both belief and action—turning from death to life.

Numbers 21 tells a similar story, though on a far greater scale. The people of Israel, weary and resentful, complained against God's provision. In response, he sent fiery serpents whose venom burned like fire. Death slithered through the camp until the people confessed their sin. But God didn't remove the serpents—he gave them a cure. A bronze serpent lifted on a pole became the means of life for all who would look in faith. The very image of death became a symbol of healing.

This moment in Israel's journey captures the heart of the gospel. Faith is not about escaping danger but trusting God's power to redeem it. Just as the Israelites looked to the bronze serpent, believers look to Christ "lifted up" on the cross. Healing and hope still come the same way—not by striving, but by looking to the Savior who turns curse into cure.

EXAMINATION

Victory over Arad (21:1–3)

After the sorrow of Aaron's death and the detour around Edom, Israel's morale was fragile. Yet Numbers 21 opens with a surprising burst of triumph. The Canaanite king of Arad attacked from the Negev, capturing some Israelites. The people cried out to God, promising total devotion: "If you will indeed give this people into my hand, then I will devote their cities to destruction" (21:2). For the first time in a long time, Israel responded to crisis with faith rather than complaint. The Lord granted victory, and the place was named Hormah—"destruction."

This battle, though brief, was symbolic. The nation that once refused to fight now fought and won. Faith, even when born in weakness, rekindled victory. The Lord's faithfulness, not Israel's military skill, brought success. Each small triumph along the way became a rehearsal for greater conquests in Canaan. But faith had to be sustained, not sporadic—and as the journey continued, old habits soon resurfaced.

The fiery serpents and the bronze serpent (21:4–9)

The victory over Arad faded quickly as the people grew impatient. Traveling around Edom forced them into a longer, harsher route through the wilderness. The text said, "The people became impatient on the way" (21:4). Impatience led to ingratitude, and ingratitude turned to blasphemy: "Why have you brought us up out of Egypt to die in the wilderness? For there is no food and no water, and we loathe this worthless food" (21:5). The "worthless food" was manna—the daily miracle of God's provision. Their complaint was not just about diet; it was about dependence. They were tired of living by faith.

Then the Lord sent "fiery serpents" among the people. The Hebrew phrase literally means "burning serpents," likely referring to the painful, inflammatory venom of desert vipers. The serpents became physical symbols of the inner poison of unbelief that had infected Israel's soul. The punishment was swift and terrifying: "many people of Israel died" (21:6). The wilderness that once supplied food now became a graveyard of serpents.

But even judgment became the soil for mercy. The people confessed to Moses, "We have sinned, for we have spoken against the Lord and against you" (21:7). It was one of the few times in Numbers where genuine repentance surfaced. They asked Moses to intercede, and God answered—but in an unexpected way. Instead of removing the serpents, he provided a remedy: "Make a fiery serpent and set it on a pole, and everyone who is bitten, when he sees it, shall live" (21:8).

Moses fashioned a bronze serpent and lifted it high for all to see. Those who looked at it in faith were healed. The text did not say the serpent had magical power; it was a visible sign of invisible trust. The act of looking required belief that God's promise was true. Healing came not through self-effort or ritual but through faith expressed in obedience. The cure mirrored the cause: as sin came through sight (Eve's gaze at the forbidden fruit), so salvation came through a redemptive gaze toward God's provision.

This moment stands among the most profound in Israel's wilderness story. The God who disciplines also delivers. The same serpents that brought death now became the image of salvation when lifted up in faith. Centuries later, Jesus would interpret this event for Nicodemus: "As Moses lifted up the serpent in the wilderness, so must the Son of Man be lifted up, that whoever believes in him may have eternal life" (John 3:14–15). The bronze serpent thus became a type of Christ's crucifixion—an emblem of judgment transformed into healing.

The lesson endures: faith looks upward, not inward. The Israelites could not save themselves by running from snakes or treating their wounds. They had to trust the God who turned the symbol of the curse into the source of life. In the same way, believers today find healing not by escaping the effects of sin but by looking to the One who bore sin's curse on the cross.

Songs and springs in the wilderness (21:10–20)

After the fiery serpents, the narrative shifts from despair to praise. The camp moved northward, and a surprising note of joy enters the text. Israel began to sing again. In verses 16–18, we find what scholars call the "Song of the Well."

This short hymn celebrates God's faithfulness in providing fresh water in the wilderness. The well symbolized renewal, both physical and spiritual. The same God who disciplined them with serpents now refreshed them with springs. Out of the barren desert, life flowed again. The juxtaposition of serpents and springs reinforces the book's recurring theme: God's grace followed repentance.

The mention of "princes" digging the well suggests that leadership and worship intersect when both are guided by gratitude. The people's song marked a turning point in attitude. Where they once cursed the manna, they now praised the water. The journey from complaint to song mirrored the journey of faith itself—learning to see God's goodness even in the dry places.

This passage bridges judgment and victory. The songs of Numbers 21 anticipate the songs of Canaan. They foreshadowed the worship that followed deliverance. Israel was learning that praise was not reserved for the Promised Land—it begins in the wilderness. Even before battles are won, faith sings.

Victories over Sihon and Og (21:21–35)

The chapter concludes with two decisive victories that prepared Israel for entry into Canaan. Having circled Edom, the nation encountered King Sihon of the Amorites. Moses requested peaceful passage, echoing his earlier appeal to Edom: "Let me pass through your land; we will not turn aside into field or vineyard" (21:22). Sihon refused and marched out to fight. But this time, there was no panic, no grumbling, no retreat. Israel defeated him and occupied his territory from the Arnon to the Jabbok.

The conquest was so significant that the text quoted a Canaanite victory poem—ironically celebrating Sihon's earlier triumph over Moab—to highlight God's reversal of fortunes. The nations' songs of pride now became Israel's songs of praise. The land once ruled by enemies became the foothold of faith. The Lord had turned the wilderness wanderers into warriors.

Next came King Og of Bashan, whose stature and strongholds intimidated later generations (Deut. 3:11). Yet his power collapsed before God's promise. "The Lord said to Moses, 'Do not fear him, for I have given him into your hand'" (21:34). That assurance transformed fear into faith, and victory followed. By the end of the chapter, Israel controlled key regions east of the Jordan—proof that God's faithfulness not only healed but empowered.

The progression of the chapter is deliberate. It moves from defeat to victory, from death to life, from complaint to confidence. The bronze serpent represents inward healing; the battles with Sihon and Og represent outward triumph. Faith that looks to God for healing becomes the faith that trusts him for victory. The one who saved from serpents can also subdue kings.

Together, these stories form a miniature gospel. Sin brings death, faith brings life, gratitude restores joy, and trust leads to triumph. The God who judged Israel for unbelief now strengthened them through faith. What began with fiery serpents ended with flowing springs and fallen kings. Grace did not erase the wilderness—it redeemed it.

The lesson for Christians is timeless. We still walk through deserts of impatience and valleys of venom. We still face the temptation to look down at our wounds rather than up at our Savior. But every look toward Christ—the true serpent lifted up—heals the soul. Faith is not the denial of pain; it is the decision to see beyond it.

Numbers 21 marks a turning point not just in geography but in theology. The people who once cursed the manna now sang at the well. The nation that once feared giants now conquered kings. All of it flowed from one act of faith—one upward glance toward God's provision. The wilderness was no longer a place of death but a classroom of grace.

APPLICATION

1. Faith looks upward, not inward

When the serpents struck, Israel's healing came not from self-effort but from looking up. The bronze serpent lifted on the pole demanded an act of faith—trusting that God's promise, not human remedy, brought life. Many still search inward for salvation, hoping that effort, emotion, or understanding can heal the soul. But the cure for sin always comes from beyond us. Just as Israel had to look up, we must fix their eyes on Christ, "lifted up" on the cross. Faith begins when self-reliance ends. The gospel invites us to raise our gaze from wounds to the One who was wounded for us. Our greatest need is not deliverance from pain but restoration of sight—the vision to see that God alone can heal.

2. Complaining blinds us to grace

Israel's venom began long before the snakes—it started with grumbling. Complaint always narrows the soul's vision. When we fixate on what we lack, we lose sight of what God has already given. The people called manna "worthless food," forgetting it was bread from heaven. Their ingratitude turned nourishment into nausea. The same pattern still poisons hearts today. Murmuring blinds us to mercy, and discontent breeds distrust. Yet God's response was astonishing: he transformed the very image of judgment into a means of grace. Every believer who looks to Christ sees the same miracle—God turning our sin into the stage for his salvation. Gratitude reopens our eyes to grace. When we thank him for what seems small, we begin to see again the wonders of his faithfulness.

3. Healing comes through faith, not avoidance

When the serpents swarmed, God didn't remove them; he provided a remedy. That distinction matters. Sometimes Christians want deliverance without transformation—we pray for problems to vanish rather than for hearts to be renewed. But God often heals by teaching us to trust in the midst of trial. Israel had to look at the very image of what had harmed them to find healing. Likewise, repentance requires facing sin honestly, not running from it. The cross confronts us with the reality of judgment, yet also reveals the depth of mercy. The faith that looks to Christ does not deny pain; it endures it with hope. Healing begins not when circumstances change, but when trust does. God's grace doesn't always remove the serpents, but it always restores the soul.

4. Faith in God today prepares us for victory tomorrow

The chapter that begins with serpents ends with songs and victories. The people who looked up in faith later marched forward in confidence. Trusting God for healing became the training ground for trusting him in battle. The same progression marks the life of every believer. Faith learned in crisis becomes strength for calling. When we fix our eyes on God amid affliction, we learn that his faithfulness extends beyond the wound. Israel's conquests over Sihon and Og show that healed people become courageous people. The Lord who restores the heart also equips the hands. Looking to him for mercy today builds the faith to follow him into future victories. The gaze that heals is the same gaze that conquers.

CONCLUSION

Numbers 21 begins with complaint and ends with conquest—a story that moves from poison to praise. Israel's healing did not come through effort or escape but through faith that looked up to God's provision. The bronze serpent lifted high became a testimony that grace can triumph even in judgment. Centuries later, Jesus revealed that this ancient symbol pointed to his own cross, where sin's curse was turned into salvation. Faith still works the same way today: those who look to Christ live. The wilderness may still sting, but God's mercy still heals. When hearts lift their eyes to him, the venom of sin gives way to the victory of grace.

REFLECTION

1. Why was Israel's impatience such a serious form of unbelief in God's goodness?

2. What does the bronze serpent teach about the nature of faith and God's healing?

3. How does God's decision to heal rather than remove the serpents reveal his wisdom?

4. Why is gratitude a necessary antidote to grumbling in the life of faith?

5. How do the songs and victories later in the chapter flow from Israel's renewed trust?

6. In what ways does Christ fulfill the meaning of the serpent lifted up in the wilderness?

DISCUSSION

1. How can we cultivate the habit of "looking up" to God instead of focusing inward on pain?

2. What does this story teach about how God transforms judgment into grace?

3. How do modern believers experience "fiery serpents" of sin or discouragement today?

4. What practical disciplines help us move from complaint to contentment?

5. How does the faith that brings healing also prepare us for spiritual battle?

6. Why is it vital to remember that healing and salvation both depend entirely on God's provision?

8

BALAAM & THE BLESSINGS OF GOD

NUMBERS 22–25

Objective: To show that God's sovereign purpose prevails even through human greed, corruption, and rebellion.

INTRODUCTION

During World War II, Allied forces famously turned one of Hitler's greatest spies into a double agent. The man, code-named Garbo, fed German intelligence just enough truth to appear credible—while secretly serving the Allies. His reports misled the Nazis into defending the wrong beaches on D-Day, ensuring the success of the Normandy invasion. The irony is unforgettable: the enemy's own agent became the instrument of their defeat.

Numbers 22–25 tells a story just as astonishing. Balak, king of Moab, hires the pagan prophet Balaam to curse Israel. He spares no expense, believing that money can buy divine power. But the God of Israel cannot be manipulated. Instead of curses, Balaam's lips deliver blessings—and even prophecies of the coming Messiah. Yet the tale doesn't end with victory alone. Balaam's greed and Moab's cunning later lead Israel into idolatry, proving that corruption always lurks near blessing. Through it all, God's sovereignty shines. Every human scheme—Balak's fear, Balaam's greed, Israel's lust—is bent to fulfill divine purpose.

This narrative reminds believers that God's rule is absolute. He can turn enemies into instruments, corruption into confirmation, and even rebellion into revelation. Human failure may complicate God's story, but it can never cancel it. The God who overruled Balaam's curse still turns darkness into blessing for those who trust him.

EXAMINATION

Balak's fear and Balaam's summons (22:1–20)

Israel's victories over Sihon and Og sent shockwaves across Moab. King Balak, watching from the plains east of the Jordan, saw the approaching nation as an existential threat. "This horde will lick up all that is around us, as the ox licks up the grass of the field" (22:4). Fear, not faith, drove his next move. Rather than seek peace or humility before Israel's God, Balak turned to manipulation. He hired a prophet-for-profit named Balaam to curse God's people.

Balaam, a well-known diviner from Pethor near the Euphrates, was famous for his reputation—someone who could bless or curse with supernatural power. His name itself may have meant "devourer" or "destroyer of people," suggesting spiritual potency in the ancient world's eyes. Balak's strategy was political and spiritual: if he could not defeat Israel's sword, perhaps he could undermine their blessing. What he didn't understand was that the blessing wasn't Israel's to manipulate—it belonged to God.

When Balak's envoys arrived with gifts and promises of payment, Balaam initially appeared pious: "I must wait to hear what the Lord will say to me." But his words masked divided motives. He called Israel "the people who came out of Egypt," avoiding acknowledgment of their divine calling. God's first response was clear: "You shall not go with them. You shall not curse the people, for they are blessed" (22:12). The matter should have ended there, but greed refused to die easily.

Balak sent a second delegation with greater prestige and richer promises. This time, Balaam's hesitation betrayed his heart. He invited the men to stay the night again, as though God might revise his command for the right price. God permitted Balaam to go—but only to speak what he was told. The prophet got what he wanted—a journey to Moab—but not the autonomy he craved. Already, the lesson was forming: human corruption might scheme and bargain, but God's sovereignty stood unaltered.

The angel and the talking donkey (22:21-41)

Balaam's greed soon met divine irony. As he rode toward Moab, God's anger burned because his journey, though permitted, sprang from impure motives. The Angel of the Lord blocked the path with a drawn sword. Balaam, blinded by ambition, didn't see him—but his donkey did. Three times the animal turned aside, saving its master's life. Three times Balaam beat it in frustration.

Then the Lord opened the donkey's mouth. "What have I done to you, that you have struck me these three times?" (22:28). The humor of the moment was deliberate and devastating. The "seer" could not see, while his donkey perceived the divine messenger. Balaam's spiritual blindness exposed his moral blindness. He could speak to kings but could not discern when he was opposing God.

When the angel finally revealed himself, Balaam fell facedown, confessing, "I have sinned." Yet his repentance was partial—motivated by fear, not faith. The angel repeated God's condition: "Go with the men, but speak only the word that I tell you" (22:35). God would use even a compromised prophet to proclaim uncorrupted truth. The episode with the donkey underlines this theme: God's sovereignty extends even to animals and angels. Nothing—not greed, pride, or ignorance—can derail his purpose.

When Balaam arrived, Balak greeted him with impatience and flattery: "Did I not send to you to call you? Am I not able to honor you?" (22:37). The king expected control, but Balaam uttered a prophetic disclaimer that frames the rest of the story: "The word that God puts in my mouth, that must I speak" (22:38). The stage was set for a battle between divine sovereignty and human manipulation.

Balaam's oracles of blessing (23:1-24:25)

Balak escorted Balaam to high places overlooking Israel's camp—first at Bamoth-baal, then Pisgah, then Peor. At each site, altars were built, sacrifices were offered, and expectations were raised. Balak believed location and ritual might sway divine favor, but God could not be bribed. Instead of curses, blessings poured out.

First oracle (23:1-12): Balaam began with theological clarity: "How can I curse whom God has not cursed?" The prophet blessed Israel as a people set apart, numbering like the dust of the earth. The astonished king protested, "What have you done to me?" but Balaam replied simply, "Must I not take care to speak what the Lord puts in my mouth?"

Second oracle (23:13-26): Balak tried again from another vantage point, thinking perhaps a new perspective would produce a new result. Balaam, however, repeated and expanded the blessing: "God is not man, that he should lie, or a son of man, that he should change his mind" (23:19). The declaration struck at the heart of Balak's superstition. Human curses can shift with bribes, but divine promises stand fixed. Israel's victory was certain because it rested on God's unchanging nature.

Third oracle (24:1-9): By then, Balaam no longer sought omens; he simply allowed the Spirit of God to fill him. His eyes opened—not to greed, but to glory: "How lovely are your tents, O Jacob!" The blessing culminated in a picture of Israel flourishing like gardens by rivers and trees planted by the Lord. The imagery recalled Eden restored—life under divine favor.

Fourth oracle (24:15-24): The final vision looked beyond Balaam's day to the coming of a royal deliverer: "A star shall come out of Jacob, and a scepter shall rise out of Israel." The prophecy pointed forward to David's victories and, ultimately, to the Messiah who conquered sin and death. Thus, the mouth hired to curse became the mouth that announced Christ's coming. God's sovereignty not only frustrated corruption—it transformed it into proclamation.

Each oracle reinforced the same truth: no power, pagan or prophetic, could overturn God's blessing. God's covenant word is unassailable; every attempt to manipulate it only magnifies his glory. The more Balak insisted on cursing, the more God multiplied blessing. Human corruption became the raw material of divine sovereignty.

The seduction at Peor (25:1-18)

The narrative's tone shifts abruptly. As Balaam exits the stage, Israel camped at Shittim. There, Moabite women invited the men of Israel to their feasts—and to their idols. "The people ate and bowed down to their gods" (25:2). What military and magical attacks could not achieve, seduction accomplished. The nation fell into immorality and idolatry, provoking God's anger. A plague swept through the camp, claiming twenty-four thousand lives.

Though Balaam's role is not described here, later texts (Num. 31:16; Rev. 2:14) reveal that he instigated this scheme. Unable to curse Israel directly, he advised corrupting them through temptation. It was strategy by subversion: if God could not be bribed to turn against his people, perhaps his people could be enticed to turn against God. Yet even this backdoor betrayal fell under divine control. God responded not with annihilation but with purification.

Phinehas, the grandson of Aaron, acted decisively, executing a couple engaged in public immorality. His zeal halted the plague, and God commended him: "He was jealous with my jealousy among them… therefore I give him my covenant of peace" (25:11–12). The story ends where it began—with God asserting sovereignty over sin. Balaam's corruption and Moab's cunning could not undo God's covenant. Through one faithful priest, holiness was restored.

The Balaam narrative reveals the paradox of divine sovereignty: God allowed rebellion yet overruled it; he permitted corruption yet transformed it into confirmation of his promises. Every human scheme—Balak's fear, Balaam's greed, Israel's lust—became a dark canvas upon which divine faithfulness shone brighter.

This story also exposes the limits of religious performance. Balaam could speak for God yet did not belong to him. His mouth uttered truth while his heart pursued profit. He stood as a warning that spiritual giftedness is no substitute for spiritual obedience. God can use corrupt instruments to accomplish perfect purposes, but those instruments remain accountable for their motives.

At the same time, the narrative overflows with hope. The God who turns curses into blessings and halts plagues through zeal remains sovereign over corruption today. His purposes in Christ advance through the frailty of the church, the failures of leaders, and the hostility of nations. Human sin might distort, delay, and destroy, but it can not dethrone the Lord.

APPLICATION

1. God's plans cannot be bought or blocked

Balak believed he could hire divine favor the way he hired a prophet. But no amount of money or influence can manipulate the will of God. His sovereignty stands untouched by human scheming. Balaam's greed could not cancel God's covenant, and Balak's curses became blessings instead. The same principle holds true today: corruption, politics, and power cannot overturn what God has decreed. His purposes do not depend on moral perfection or human permission. This truth humbles both kings and prophets. We do not control God; we trust him. Faith means resting in the certainty that his promises prevail, even when circumstances—or people—oppose them. When we see chaos in the world or compromise in the church, we remember that God's throne remains unshaken.

2. God can use even corrupt people to accomplish holy purposes

Balaam was not a faithful servant, yet God used his mouth to proclaim truth. His oracles foretold Israel's blessing and even the coming of the Messiah. God's sovereignty is so complete that he can employ unwilling instruments for divine ends. This doesn't excuse corruption, but it does magnify God's control. The same Lord who spoke through Balaam's donkey can speak through flawed people and imperfect preachers today. Christians should never confuse usefulness with holiness. The real test of faith is not whether God works through us, but whether we submit to him. God's sovereignty redeems even what humans misuse, turning greed into prophecy and rebellion into revelation. His word is unstoppable—pure even when the messenger is not.

3. God's blessing must not lead to moral carelessness

Israel's fall at Peor reveals the danger of presuming upon grace. After experiencing victory and blessing, the people relaxed their vigilance. When temptation came, they traded holiness for pleasure. God's blessing is meant to inspire obedience, not license. The Christian's greatest threat often arises after success, when spiritual pride dulls discernment. Balaam couldn't curse Israel, but sin within Israel did what he could not. Corruption outside the camp cannot defeat us if we guard against corruption within. God's faithfulness is constant, but our participation in his blessing requires continued faithfulness to him. When grace abounds, humility must deepen. God's sovereignty protects his covenant; our calling is to remain pure in response to it.

4. God's zeal for holiness restores what sin destroys

When Israel's sin at Peor brought a deadly plague, one man's holy zeal stopped it. Phinehas acted not out of rage but out of reverence—he defended the honor of a holy God. His boldness preserved the covenant and restored peace. God rewarded him with "a covenant of perpetual priesthood." This episode shows that divine sovereignty never leads to passivity. God rules, but he also raises up people through whom he enacts justice and mercy. Faith in a sovereign God calls for moral courage, not complacency. In a world desensitized to sin, the church must learn again to share God's jealousy for holiness. Through faithful obedience, God renews his people and proves once more that his righteousness overcomes corruption. Holiness remains the chosen instrument of divine sovereignty.

CONCLUSION

The story of Balaam proves that God's sovereignty is unshakable. Balak tried to buy power, Balaam tried to profit from prophecy, and Israel later corrupted itself through sin—but none of it overturned God's plan. The Lord turned curses into blessings, exposed greed through a talking donkey, and restored holiness through one faithful priest. Every attempt to manipulate or oppose him only magnified his glory. God's purposes may pass through human failure, but they never fail. For believers, that truth offers both comfort and challenge: comfort, because no corruption can thwart God's will; challenge, because his faithfulness calls us to trust and obey the One whose rule no one can resist.

REFLECTION

1. How does the story of Balaam reveal that God's sovereignty cannot be manipulated?

2. Why do you think God allowed Balaam to go with Balak's men even though it angered him?

3. What lessons about spiritual blindness emerge from the story of Balaam and his donkey?

4. How does God's use of Balaam's words demonstrate his control over human corruption?

5. What does Israel's fall at Peor teach about the danger of moral compromise after blessing?

6. How does Phinehas's zeal show that holiness and faithfulness can restore a corrupted people?

DISCUSSION

1. How can Christians trust God's sovereignty when corruption and injustice seem to prevail?

2. In what ways do modern forms of "spiritual bribery" still appear in the church or society?

3. Why is it dangerous to confuse spiritual giftedness with genuine faithfulness?

4. What practices can help believers remain morally vigilant after seasons of success or blessing?

5. How can Christians reflect God's zeal for holiness without becoming self-righteous or harsh?

6. What does this episode teach us about God's ability to turn evil intentions into redemptive outcomes?

9

A NEW GENERATION

NUMBERS 26-27

Objective: To show that God faithfully prepares new generations to inherit and advance his enduring promises.

INTRODUCTION

When a relay runner nears the end of their stretch, the most critical moment isn't the sprint—it's the handoff. The success of the team depends on timing, precision, and trust. If the baton drops, years of training collapse in an instant. But when the exchange is smooth, the race continues with momentum and confidence. Numbers 26-27 captures just such a moment in Israel's story—a spiritual handoff from one generation to the next.

After forty years of wandering, the old generation was gone, and God commanded a new census. Every name called was proof that the promise still stood. The failures of the past had not cancelled God's faithfulness. As the nation prepared to enter Canaan, God ensured that each family would receive its inheritance and that faithful leadership would continue through Joshua. Even the daughters of Zelophehad, who boldly claimed their father's share, illustrate that faith, not tradition, qualifies God's heirs.

This is the turning point of Numbers: death gives way to life, and disappointment to renewal. A new people rise from the wilderness, ready to believe where their parents doubted. God's covenant has survived rebellion, delay, and discipline. Through these chapters, we learn that his promises never die with a generation—they live on in those who trust him anew.

EXAMINATION

The second census (26:1–65)

After years of wandering and loss, Numbers 26 opens with a phrase of renewal: "After the plague, the Lord said to Moses and to Eleazar… 'Take a census of all the congregation of the people of Israel.'" The last census had been conducted nearly forty years earlier at Sinai (Num. 1-4). That generation had fallen in the wilderness because of unbelief. Now, God commanded a new numbering—not of the condemned, but of those prepared to inherit the promise.

The census functioned as both a record and a revelation. Every name declared that God's covenant was still alive. Israel's disobedience had not erased God's intention. The nation may have changed faces, but not faithfulness. The total number of fighting men—601,730—closely mirrors the earlier count, demonstrating that divine judgment had not diminished divine blessing. God's promise to multiply Abraham's offspring remained intact.

This census, however, also carried a solemn echo of memory. As Moses and Eleazar moved tribe by tribe, the absence of the older names spoke louder than the new. Not one of the men counted in the first census remained, except Caleb and Joshua. The chapter closed with the reminder: "For the Lord had said of them, 'They shall die in the wilderness.'" The list became a living sermon—judgment on one generation, grace for the next.

Each tribe's count also reinforced the principle of inheritance. The forthcoming division of the land would be based on these numbers. "To the larger tribe you shall give a larger inheritance, and to the smaller tribe a smaller inheritance" (26:54). The census thus linked obedience with blessing, showing that promise and preparation went hand in hand. Before God gave the land, he organized the people. Order was not the opposite of faith—it was the expression of readiness.

One small but striking detail appears in verses 9-11. The sons of Korah, whose father led a rebellion against Moses, were specifically said to have survived. Though their ancestor perished, his descendants remained. God's grace preserved a remnant even from families marked by failure. Later, their descendants would serve as temple musicians and compose psalms of worship (Pss. 42–49, 84–88). The inclusion of that note in the census underscores the theme of new beginnings: God raised worshipers from the ashes of rebellion.

The daughters of Zelophehad (27:1-11)

Immediately following the census came a remarkable case study in faith and justice. Five sisters—Mahlah, Noah, Hoglah, Milcah, and Tirzah—approached Moses, Eleazar, and the leaders of Israel with a legal question. Their father, Zelophehad of the tribe of Manasseh, had died in the wilderness without sons. According to custom, his inheritance would have been lost to his clan. The women, however, courageously stepped forward: "Why should the name of our father be taken away... because he had no son? Give to us a possession among our father's brothers" (27:4).

Their request was revolutionary. In a patriarchal society, women rarely petitioned for property rights. Yet their appeal was not defiance but faith. They believed that God's promise of land applied to their family as much as to any man's. Their question assumed the certainty of Canaan's possession. In a generation scarred by unbelief, these women exhibited unshakable confidence that God's word would come true.

Moses brought their case before the Lord, and God affirmed their claim: "The daughters of Zelophehad are right." A new statute was established, granting daughters inheritance rights when no sons remained. God's justice proved flexible without compromising order. His law bent toward inclusion without breaking covenant boundaries. The episode not only safeguarded fairness but displayed divine compassion—proof that God's promises extended to all who trusted him, regardless of gender or circumstance.

These women foreshadowed the faith of later figures—Ruth, Mary, and others—who boldly believed God's promises against social convention. Their story bridged generations, showing that faith was the true qualification for inheritance. They stood as symbols of the new generation's readiness to receive what their fathers forfeited. Where unbelief silenced men, faith now spoke through women.

Moses' approaching death (27:12-14)

After the census and the sisters' petition, the narrative takes a somber turn. God instructed Moses to climb Mount Abarim to view the Promised Land from afar. The moment was bittersweet. Moses had led Israel for forty years, but because of his failure at Meribah—striking the rock instead of speaking to it—he would not enter the land himself. From the mountaintop, he would see the fulfillment of what he had long labored toward but not experience it firsthand.

This scene echoes earlier patriarchal moments: Abraham glimpsed the stars of promise; Moses glimpsed the land itself. In both cases, the vision affirmed that God's word stood, even when human life ran out. Moses' exclusion did not signal divine abandonment but divine integrity. God remained faithful to his holiness, even when that faithfulness cost his servant deeply.

The poignancy of this scene lay in its balance of justice and grace. God did not revoke Moses' punishment, but he still granted him sight of the land. Mercy tempered discipline. Moses' story illustrates a principle every Christian has to learn: even faithful leaders are mortal, but God's mission is immortal. The promise of inheritance transcended the lifespan of its mediators.

The appointment of Joshua (27:15-23)

What followed revealed Moses' true greatness. Rather than plead for reversal, he prayed for continuity: "Let the Lord, the God of the spirits of all flesh, appoint a man over the congregation" (27:16). His concern was not for himself but for the people. He did not ask that his name be remembered but that God's guidance remain. "That the congregation of the Lord may not be as sheep that have no shepherd" (27:17).

God answered immediately: "Take Joshua the son of Nun, a man in whom is the Spirit." Joshua had been Moses' assistant since Sinai, a faithful spy, and a courageous believer. Now he became the embodiment of the new generation's faith. God instructed Moses to lay his hand on Joshua, commission him publicly, and transfer some of his authority so that all Israel would obey. Eleazar, the new high priest, would use the Urim to confirm divine guidance, symbolizing that Joshua's leadership would operate in partnership with priestly counsel.

The ceremony represented both continuity and transition. Moses placed his hands on Joshua, not to clone himself but to confirm God's calling. Authority in God's kingdom was not inherited by bloodline or ambition; it was bestowed by divine appointment and affirmed through faithful mentorship. The laying on of hands bridged generations, ensuring that God's presence would continue to lead.

Joshua's appointment highlights another crucial truth: leadership changes, but God's faithfulness does not. The God who called Moses from the bush now commissioned Joshua for the battlefield. The people who once followed pillars of fire would soon follow a man filled with the Spirit. The same promise carried them forward, now entrusted to new hands.

This passage anticipated the New Testament pattern of succession—Paul to Timothy, Elijah to Elisha, Jesus to the apostles. Each transition reminds us that God's work does not end with any single servant. The greatest leaders prepare for their own replacement, not their own remembrance. Moses' final act was to ensure that the flock had a shepherd. His willingness to step aside in obedience became the final testimony of his faith.

Through these chapters, the theme of renewal emerges with clarity: God was preparing a new generation for promise. The census established the people's readiness; the daughters of Zelophehad displayed personal faith; Moses' mountaintop moment affirmed divine consistency; and Joshua's commissioning ensured future leadership. The wilderness had done its refining work. The unbelief of the fathers had been buried, and hope rose in their children.

Numbers 26–27 forms a hinge in Israel's story. Judgment gave way to preparation, despair to expectation. The people once counted for death were now counted for inheritance. The God who disciplined also delivered; the One who buried the old raised up the new.

For the church today, the lesson endures. God continues to prepare new generations to carry his promises forward. When one era ends, another begins—not because people are strong, but because God is faithful. His covenant moved steadily toward fulfillment, one census, one leader, and one generation at a time.

APPLICATION

1. God's promises outlive every generation

The census in Numbers 26 reminds us that human generations rise and fall, but God's word remains constant. The wilderness graves of the first generation did not bury the covenant. Even after judgment, God counted his people again—a new start with the same promise. Every Christian and every church must learn this rhythm: God's mission does not depend on one era, one leader, or one people group. When faith falters in one generation, God raises another. His plans outlive our failures. This truth humbles us to serve faithfully while we can and encourages us that his story continues beyond our lifetime. The gospel never retires with its servants; it always finds new hearts to believe, new voices to proclaim, and new lives to lead.

2. Faith is the qualification for inheritance

The daughters of Zelophehad stand as examples of bold, obedient faith. They believed God's promise so completely that they petitioned for land they had never seen. Their confidence contrasted sharply with the unbelief of their fathers. Faith, not privilege, positioned them for blessing. God honored their courage and established new precedent through their trust. Their story reminds the church that inheritance is not reserved for the powerful or prominent but for those who take God at his word. True heirs of promise are not identified by status or gender but by faith that claims what God has promised. In every generation, God delights to work through those who dare to believe that his word is enough.

3. God's discipline refines; it does not abandon

Moses' inability to enter Canaan seems tragic, but it reveals God's consistency. He disciplines those he loves in order to display his holiness, yet he still fulfills his purpose through them. Moses saw the land even if he couldn't enter it, proving that divine correction does not equal rejection. In the same way, God's discipline in our lives is redemptive, not punitive. He corrects to cleanse, prunes to produce, and refines to renew. Believers often view discipline as disqualification, but Scripture views it as preparation. God's faithfulness means he will finish his work even through our flaws.

The leader who fell short still passed the baton, and the promise advanced. Grace ensures that divine purpose always moves forward, even through our failures.

4. Leadership changes, but God's faithfulness remains

The transfer of authority from Moses to Joshua highlights how God sustains his mission through changing leadership. Moses' humility in commissioning his successor displays maturity that every generation of leaders must emulate. True faith prepares for continuity, not control. The church must cultivate the same trust—believing that God will raise faithful hands when ours can no longer lead. Every spiritual transition should be an act of worship, not anxiety. God's Spirit rests on the next servant as surely as it did on the last. Leadership is temporary, but the Lord's presence is permanent. As long as God remains with his people, the mission never falters. His work outlives us, and his promises march on through those he prepares next.

CONCLUSION

Numbers 26–27 stands as a testament to God's patient faithfulness. The wilderness generation may have fallen, but God's promise rose again in their children. Through the census, the inheritance laws, and Joshua's commissioning, we see that divine purpose is never stalled by human failure. God always prepares new hearts to believe and new hands to serve. Moses' humility, the daughters' courage, and Joshua's obedience all signal that the future of God's people rests not on human strength but on divine continuity. Every generation must rediscover that truth: the God who began the work will complete it, raising up new servants to carry his promises forward.

REFLECTION

1. How does the new census in Numbers 26 reveal both God's judgment and his mercy?

2. What does the story of the daughters of Zelophehad teach about faith and inheritance?

3. Why is it significant that the sons of Korah survived and served as future worship leaders?

4. How does Moses' view of the Promised Land balance divine justice with divine grace?

5. What qualities made Joshua the right leader for a new generation?

6. How do these chapters show that God's purposes continue even when leaders or generations fail?

DISCUSSION

1. What lessons can the church learn about preparing the next generation for leadership and faithfulness?

2. How can Christians today demonstrate the same confidence in God's promises as the daughters of Zelophehad?

3. Why is spiritual succession—training and mentoring others—essential to God's ongoing mission?

4. How can we accept God's discipline as part of his faithfulness rather than as rejection?

5. What does Numbers 26-27 teach about balancing humility and responsibility in leadership transitions?

6. How can we ensure that our faith today strengthens the faith of those who come after us?

10

SACRIFICES, VOWS, & VENGEANCE

NUMBERS 28–31

Objective: To show that true faithfulness unites worship, integrity, and obedience under God's sovereign direction.

INTRODUCTION

A symphony orchestra can't succeed on passion alone. Each musician must follow the score, stay in rhythm, and trust the conductor's lead. A single offbeat note can jar the harmony. But when every section—strings, brass, percussion—moves together under the baton, the result is breathtaking. Israel's life with God was meant to sound that way. Worship, words, and warfare were all instruments in one grand composition of faithfulness.

Numbers 28–31 reminded the new generation that life in the Promised Land would demand more than zeal; it would require rhythm, integrity, and obedience. God began with the offerings, teaching that every day and every season must revolve around his presence. Then he instructed them about vows, calling for honesty in speech. Finally, he commanded judgment on Midian, showing that holiness must be defended in action as well as declared in worship.

Through altar, word, and battle, God formed a people whose devotion touched every corner of life. Faithfulness is not a weekend performance but a lifelong discipline. The one who worships sincerely must also speak truthfully and live obediently. These chapters call believers today to the same harmony—to live as a symphony of faith, where worship shapes words, words guide actions, and every note exalts the God who conducts it all.

EXAMINATION

The rhythm of worship (28:1–29:40)

As Israel stood poised on the edge of Canaan, God turned their attention from conquest to consistency. The land ahead would be filled with battles, but before swords were drawn, God commanded sacrifices. Numbers 28–29 repeats many of the offerings already described in Leviticus, but here the emphasis is not on atonement—it is on rhythm. Worship had to become the heartbeat of national life. Faithfulness was measured not only by courage in war but by constancy at the altar.

God began with daily offerings—two lambs each day, morning and evening, accompanied by grain and drink offerings. These represented continual dependence. Worship was not an occasional event but a way of life. Israel's day began and ended with remembrance of God's presence. The weekly Sabbath added a layer of rest and renewal, reminding the people that work was holy only when framed by worship.

Next came the monthly offerings tied to the new moon, marking Israel's time as sacred. Their calendar, like their camp, revolved around God. Every new month began with sacrifice, acknowledging that time itself belonged to the Creator. Festivals such as Passover, Weeks, Trumpets, the Day of Atonement, and Tabernacles followed. Each feast punctuated the year with celebration and surrender. These rhythms wove worship into every season—harvests, rest, repentance, and rejoicing.

This repetition of sacrificial instructions served as a covenant renewal for the new generation. The previous generation had learned worship at Sinai; this one would practice it in the land. Worship in the Promised Land would remind them daily that victory did not come from military strength but from spiritual devotion.

The magnitude of these offerings might seem overwhelming—bulls, rams, lambs, flour, oil, and wine—but they taught an essential truth: gratitude always cost something. Faithfulness was not cheap. God's repeated refrain, "You shall offer to me at its appointed time," anchors the section. Obedience in worship trained the heart to trust God's timing in everything else.

These chapters also highlight communal unity. The priests, Levites, and tribes cooperated to ensure that worship never ceased. Faithfulness at the altar sustained faithfulness in the camp. The people who offered daily sacrifices would later march with daily confidence. The altar was the foundation for every victory to come.

Integrity in vows (30:1–16)

From the altar, God turned to the word. Numbers 30 addresses the making and keeping of vows. Faithfulness before God involved not only what they offered but also what they said. A vow was a voluntary promise—a commitment of devotion, sacrifice, or abstinence made to the Lord. God took such promises seriously: "If a man vows a vow to the Lord… he shall not break his word. He shall do according to all that proceeds out of his mouth" (30:2).

The text then distinguishes between vows made by men and women, reflecting the patriarchal structure of ancient Israel. A husband or father could annul a woman's vow if it affected family obligations, but only if he acted immediately. Silence signified consent; hesitation sealed the promise. While these regulations might sound distant to modern ears, their purpose was protection, not oppression. They ensured that vows were deliberate, not impulsive, and that authority carried responsibility for oversight.

The deeper principle applies universally: words matter because they reflect character. God's people have to mirror the God who always keeps his word. Broken promises, careless oaths, and empty commitments dishonor his name. Jesus echoed this when he said, "Let your 'Yes' be yes and your 'No' be no" (Matt. 5:37).

This chapter forms a bridge between the sacrifices of chapters 28–29 and the warfare of chapter 31. Faithfulness in private speech prepared for faithfulness in public action. Before Israel waged war, God ensured that their tongues and consciences were aligned with holiness. A people who spoke truth before God could stand firm against enemies before men.

Vengeance on Midian (31:1–54)

The final chapter of this section presents one of the most sobering episodes in Numbers. God commanded Moses, "Avenge the people of Israel on the Midianites. Afterward you shall be gathered to your people" (31:2). This was Moses' last military act—a divine directive of judgment against those who led Israel into idolatry at Peor. The battle was not for expansion but for purification. The Midianites had seduced Israel through immorality and false worship; now God's justice required reckoning.

Twelve thousand soldiers—one thousand from each tribe—were chosen for the campaign. Eleazar's son Phinehas, whose zeal once stopped the plague at Peor, went with them, carrying the holy vessels and trumpets of alarm. The presence of sacred objects among the soldiers underscored that this was holy war, not human revenge. The mission was to uphold God's holiness, not satisfy Israel's pride.

The campaign was swift and decisive. The text reports that the Israelites killed the Midianite kings and Balaam, who had counseled the seduction at Peor. Yet when the soldiers returned, Moses was angered that they had spared the women who had caused Israel's downfall. His rebuke reminded them that holiness demands completeness. The command to purify the spoils—passing metals through fire and washing garments in water—reinforced the same principle: even victory had to be sanctified. God's people could not bring contamination back into the camp.

The chapter concludes with meticulous distribution of the plunder. Half was given to the soldiers and half to the rest of Israel, with a portion from each dedicated to the Lord and the priests. This careful accounting transformed warfare into worship. Faithfulness required stewardship even in triumph. The soldiers' voluntary offering of additional gold to the tabernacle—"to make atonement for ourselves before the Lord" (31:50)—proved that their hearts remained reverent. They recognized that even success could corrupt if not surrendered to God.

The theological tension in this chapter is undeniable. Modern readers struggle with the violence of divine vengeance. Yet within Israel's covenant context, the Midianite campaign was not ethnic extermination but moral purification. It answered a specific act of treachery meant to destroy Israel's identity as God's holy nation. Unchecked evil corrodes God's people from within. Holiness sometimes requires hard obedience.

This chapter mirrors the same divine order seen in the sacrifices and vows. In every sphere—worship, word, and warfare—faithfulness means aligning human actions with God's purpose. The battle against Midian was the external expression of the internal struggle against sin. The same zeal that purged idolatry from the camp had to continue in the heart.

Faithfulness woven through altar, word, and battle

Taken together, these chapters revealed a comprehensive theology of faithfulness. God called his people to consistency in devotion, integrity in speech, and obedience in action. Worship without truth became hypocrisy; truth without obedience became arrogance. Faithfulness was whole-life loyalty to God.

At the altar, Israel learned dependence—daily, weekly, monthly, and yearly rhythms that centered life on God's grace. Through vows, they learned integrity—words spoken before the Lord had to reflect his character. In battle, they learned obedience—victory came not through might but through holiness. Each sphere reflected a facet of covenant faithfulness.

God's sovereignty tied them all together. He provided the sacrifices, regulated the vows, and directed the warfare. The people's task was to respond with trust and discipline. Faithfulness in one area reinforced the others. Worship strengthened integrity; integrity fueled courage; courage safeguarded holiness.

By commanding sacrifices on the eve of Canaan's conquest, God taught that the greatest victories began in devotion, not in strategy. By legislating vows, he ensured that promises mirrored his truthfulness. By ordering judgment on Midian, he reminded Israel that purity was essential to possessing the promise. The God who demanded faithfulness in worship was the same God who empowered faithfulness in war.

For modern believers, these chapters offer a challenge and a comfort. God still calls his people to faithfulness in every sphere—on Sundays at the altar, on weekdays in words, and in the battles of everyday obedience. Our worship has to shape our speech; our speech has to guide our actions; and our actions have to reflect our allegiance to the Lord. The rhythm of sacrifice, the integrity of vows, and the courage of holy obedience forms a single melody of faithfulness.

As Numbers 28–31 closes, the wilderness journey nears its end. Israel stood ready to enter the land, not just armed for battle but anchored in devotion. God had transformed a wandering people into a worshiping, speaking, and acting community of faith. Through altar, word, and warfare, he had prepared them to live as his covenant people in a promised place.

APPLICATION

1. Faithfulness begins at the altar

Before Israel marched into battle, God reminded them to keep the daily offerings. Victory begins not with swords but with surrender. Faithfulness at the altar anchors every other form of obedience. The sacrifices in Numbers 28-29 established a rhythm that kept worship central and gratitude continual. For Christians, the altar has been fulfilled in Christ, yet the rhythm remains—daily dependence, thanksgiving, and praise. When worship becomes irregular, faithfulness in other areas soon falters. Every day we must return to the altar of grace, remembering that we live by the mercy of God, not the might of our hands. Spiritual renewal always starts where we kneel before God. Only a people faithful in worship can remain faithful in battle.

2. Integrity in words proves loyalty to God

Numbers 30 shows that vows, promises, and commitments matter deeply to God. He is truth, and his people must reflect his reliability. Faithfulness in speech is worship with the tongue. Whether we make formal vows or simple promises, integrity reveals our trust in God's character. When we keep our word even at a cost, we mirror his faithfulness to us. In a culture where words are disposable and commitments are flexible, disciples must reclaim the holiness of honesty. Every promise we make—before God, family, or church—becomes an altar of trust. Breaking it dishonors the God whose promises never fail. Faithfulness is measured not only by the songs we sing but by the sentences we keep.

3. Obedience in battle demonstrates holiness in action

The war against Midian was not about conquest but cleansing. It tested whether Israel would obey when obedience was hard. Faithfulness in worship and speech prepared them for faithfulness in warfare. The same God who accepted their sacrifices and vows commanded their discipline against evil. For Christians, the battle today is spiritual, not physical, yet the principle endures: holiness requires decisive action. Compromise with sin always leads to corruption. Faith is proven not by what we feel but by what we choose when obedience costs something. God calls his people to confront what defiles them—habits, idols, or influences—with the same zeal that drove Phinehas to defend holiness. True faith fights for purity, not for power.

4. Faithfulness must permeate all of life

Numbers 28–31 portrays faithfulness as comprehensive, not compartmentalized. Worship, words, and warfare are not separate arenas but one integrated calling. The God who receives offerings is the same God who governs our speech and directs our actions. Faithfulness is a lifestyle, not a location. We cannot honor God in worship while lying in speech or compromising in conduct. Integrity must flow from the sanctuary into every conversation and every confrontation. The rhythm of sacrifice trains the heart to honor God in the ordinary; the keeping of vows disciplines the soul to trust him in adversity. Faithfulness everywhere begins with faithfulness somewhere. When God reigns at the altar, he rules over every word and every battle that follows.

CONCLUSION

Numbers 28–31 portrays a faith that touches every part of life—altar, word, and battlefield. The God who commands daily worship also demands honest speech and courageous obedience. Faithfulness is not fragmented devotion but wholehearted loyalty that honors him in every sphere. Israel learned that victory in war and stability in worship both flow from the same source: trust in God's holiness. For Christians today, this passage calls us to live in rhythm with God's will—consistent in prayer, truthful in speech, and obedient in action. When our lives echo his order, the result is harmony, not chaos, and our faith becomes the melody through which the world hears God's steadfast faithfulness.

REFLECTION

1. How do the daily, weekly, and yearly sacrifices in Numbers 28–29 teach the value of consistency in worship?

2. Why does God link integrity in vows to faithfulness in relationship with him?

3. What does the war against Midian reveal about the seriousness of sin and the necessity of holiness?

4. How does faithfulness in small, repeated acts of obedience prepare us for larger tests of faith?

5. Why is it important to see worship, speech, and obedience as one unified expression of faith?

6. How can believers today maintain spiritual balance between reverent worship and active obedience?

DISCUSSION

1. What rhythms or disciplines help you maintain daily faithfulness at your own "altar" of devotion?

2. How can Christians ensure that their words carry the same reliability as God's promises?

3. What dangers arise when worship becomes disconnected from everyday integrity or morality?

4. In what ways can believers "wage war" against sin in their own lives with holiness and humility?

5. How does Numbers 28–31 challenge Christians to view faith as an all-encompassing lifestyle?

6. What practical steps can a congregation take to cultivate faithfulness across worship, word, and action?

11

THE TRANSJORDAN TRIBES

NUMBERS 32

Objective: To show that genuine faithfulness surrenders self-interest for the sake of God's greater mission.

INTRODUCTION

In 1848, a group of pioneers known as the Donner Party set out for California. Midway through their journey, they found lush meadows near the Great Salt Lake and debated whether to stop or continue. The land seemed good, the cattle were weary, and the mountains ahead looked daunting. Some argued that safety and comfort were better than risk and hardship. Those who stayed never reached the promise of the Pacific; those who pressed on endured hardship but found what they were seeking. The tension between comfort and calling has tested travelers ever since.

Reuben and Gad faced a similar dilemma in Numbers 32. They saw the rich pastures east of the Jordan and asked Moses to let them settle there instead of crossing into Canaan. Their reasoning was logical, but their request revealed a deeper struggle: the pull between self-interest and communal faithfulness. Moses' rebuke forced them to choose whether they would live for personal gain or shared mission. In the end, they pledged to fight alongside their brothers before returning to their herds.

This episode reminds Christians that God calls us not to convenience but to cooperation. Faithfulness sometimes means crossing the river when staying put seems easier. True obedience places the good of God's people above personal comfort.

EXAMINATION

The request for the Transjordan land (32:1–5)

The book of Numbers began with a census and ends with choices. As Israel prepared to cross the Jordan and claim the land of promise, two tribes—Reuben and Gad—saw opportunity before them. The pastures east of the river, in the territory of Gilead and Jazer, were ideal for livestock. The text noted that they had "a very great number of cattle," and so they approached Moses, Eleazar, and the leaders with a bold proposal: "If we have found favor in your sight, let this land be given to your servants for a possession. Do not take us across the Jordan" (32:5).

At first glance, their request seemed practical. God had already delivered these territories from the Amorite kings Sihon and Og. The land was fertile, defensible, and available. Why not settle where success had already been achieved? Yet beneath the surface lay a dangerous temptation—to stop short of God's full promise. Reuben and Gad were not rebelling, but they were redefining the boundaries of obedience. What God intended as a foothold for conquest, they viewed as a finish line.

The passage invites reflection on the subtle pull of self-interest. The tribes' reasoning was agricultural, not theological. Their focus was on what benefited their herds, not what blessed the nation. Comfort began to compete with calling. Faith rarely fails in the face of giants; it often falters in the presence of green pastures. Their request exposed a perennial tension: how to enjoy God's blessings without using them as an excuse to avoid further obedience.

Moses' rebuke and warning (32:6–15)

Moses' reaction was swift and sharp. His tone revealed more than irritation—it echoed the trauma of an old wound. "Shall your brothers go to the war while you sit here?" (32:6). The words immediately recalled the faithless generation at Kadesh-barnea, who refused to enter the land after the spies' discouraging report. Moses saw history threatening to repeat itself. He warned that their hesitation could "discourage the heart of the people," spreading fear like a contagion.

The parallel is deliberate. Just as unbelief once delayed Israel's inheritance by forty years, selfishness now threatened to divide it. Moses reviewed the nation's painful past: "Your fathers did this, when I sent them from Kadesh-barnea to see the land… and the Lord's anger was kindled that day." The older generation died in the desert because of disunity; would the new one repeat the same sin in a different form?

Moses' rebuke reveals a profound understanding of communal faithfulness. In God's covenant, no tribe or believer stands alone. The promise was given to the whole people, and the mission required collective obedience. To pursue personal security at the expense of shared calling was to betray both God and neighbor. The rebuke also exposed how easily self-interest could masquerade as wisdom. Reuben and Gad were not faithless cowards; they were practical realists. Yet Moses reminded them that pragmatism without participation undermined God's purpose.

His warning reached beyond the ancient plains of Moab. The church today faces the same temptation—to prioritize comfort over mission, security over sacrifice. Moses' question still convicted: "Shall your brothers go to war while you sit here?" Faith that sought blessing without burden fractured the community of God.

The tribes' vow of cooperation (32:16–27)

To their credit, the tribes of Reuben and Gad listened. Their reply transformed the conversation from self-centeredness to shared responsibility. They proposed a compromise: they would build enclosures for their livestock and fortified towns for their families east of the Jordan, but they themselves would cross over "armed before the Lord" to fight alongside their brothers until every tribe received its inheritance. Only then would they return to settle their own land.

Their words reflected both repentance and resolve. The phrase "before the Lord" appears repeatedly, signaling a renewed awareness that their duty was not merely to Moses or Israel but to God himself. They no longer defined faithfulness by location but by participation. What began as a request to stay behind became a pledge to stand with.

Moses accepted their offer but added accountability: "If you will do this… then afterward you shall return, and you shall be free of obligation to the Lord and to Israel" (32:20–22). The condition was clear—obedience had to be complete, or the arrangement collapsed. Moses' warning was blunt: "Be sure your sin will find you out." The statement, often quoted apart from context, here spoke of covenant accountability. God's people could not separate private motives from public mission.

This agreement struck a delicate balance between individuality and unity. The tribes might live outside the physical boundaries of Canaan, but they had to remain spiritually bound to the nation's destiny. Faithfulness, in God's eyes, was measured not by where one lived but by how one served. Reuben and Gad modeled the redemption of self-interest through commitment. Their livestock still grazed east of the river, but their loyalty crossed westward with the ark.

This episode provides an important theological correction to both extremes: it condemns selfish isolation while affirming legitimate diversity. God's people can hold different callings and inheritances, but they must share a single mission. The tribes' vow transformed compromise into cooperation, showing that unity in purpose outweighed uniformity in position.

Moses' agreement and distribution (32:28–42)

The final section records Moses' formalization of the arrangement. He instructed Eleazar the priest, Joshua, and the tribal chiefs to ensure the agreement's fulfillment. This delegation showed that Moses' leadership, though nearing its end, remained rooted in shared governance. The covenant community would hold these tribes accountable to their word long after Moses was gone. Faithfulness had to outlast one generation's oversight.

Reuben, Gad, and half of Manasseh received the lands of Sihon and Og—the very territories Israel had conquered earlier (Num. 21). The list of towns and settlements at the chapter's end might appear routine, but it signaled permanence. What began as a tentative request ended as established inheritance. God allowed their desire because it no longer threatened unity. The tribes' commitment to fight for their brothers transformed self-interest into sanctioned blessing.

Still, the narrative closes with quiet tension. The decision was permitted, not ideal. Living east of the Jordan would later expose these tribes to isolation and vulnerability. Centuries later, during foreign invasions, they would be the first to fall (1 Chron. 5:25–26). Compromise, though sanctified, remained risky. God honored their faithfulness but did not remove the natural consequences of distance. The story thus balances grace and warning: faithfulness can redeem self-interest, but it cannot erase its dangers.

Theologically, this chapter functions as a bridge between wilderness and inheritance. It encapsulates the lessons of Numbers—the danger of disunity, the necessity of obedience, and the possibility of grace. The tribes' negotiation mirrored Israel's broader journey from rebellion to responsibility. Where their ancestors grumbled at Kadesh, they now cooperated at Gilead. Maturity replaced murmuring. The new generation learned to balance personal need with communal faith.

Faithfulness amid tension

Numbers 32 captures a truth every Christian has to face: God's people live in the tension between personal desires and collective devotion. Faithfulness rarely eliminates self-interest. Reuben and Gad teach that blessing become dangerous when it disconnects us from mission. Their initial request reflected comfort; their final commitment revealed covenant.

Moses' handling of the episode offers a model of wise leadership. He didn't reject their request outright but tested their motives, confronted their fears, and guided them toward unity. Leaders today have to exercise the same discernment—challenging selfishness while making room for sincere difference. Unity is not forced conformity; it is shared faithfulness under God's command.

Ultimately, this story points forward to a greater tension resolved in Christ. Jesus, like the faithful tribes, took on the burden of others' battles. He entered the conflict we could not win, crossing the ultimate divide to secure our inheritance. His selfless obedience transformed our self-interest into service. In him, communal faithfulness became personal calling.

Numbers 32 ends with Israel divided by geography but united by purpose. The tribes' livestock grazed in Gilead, but their hearts remained tied to the mission across the Jordan. Their story reminds every generation that faithfulness to God always demands balance—between the blessings we hold and the battles we still have to fight for others.

APPLICATION

1. Faithfulness requires balancing personal blessing with shared responsibility

Reuben and Gad teach that self-interest is not always sinful—but it must always be surrendered. Their request for land east of the Jordan was understandable; the pastures were ideal for their flocks. Yet Moses reminded them that privilege must never replace participation. God blesses us not to isolate us, but to involve us. Wealth, talent, or opportunity becomes dangerous when it detaches us from the mission of God's people. The tribes redeemed their request by committing to fight beside their brothers. Likewise, Christians must learn to hold blessings loosely and service firmly. Faithfulness does not forbid enjoyment of God's gifts, but it demands that we use them for the good of the whole body. True prosperity joins personal contentment to communal responsibility.

2. Self-interest unchecked breeds disunity

Moses' warning—"Shall your brothers go to war while you sit here?"—remains one of Scripture's most searching questions. Self-interest, if left unchecked, fractures the people of God. It whispers that comfort is more important than calling and convenience more urgent than community. In every generation, believers face the temptation to "stay east of the Jordan"—to enjoy blessings without bearing burdens. But God calls us to shared obedience, not solitary success. When the church forgets its collective mission, it repeats Israel's wilderness mistakes. The cure for disunity is not uniformity but shared sacrifice. The church flourishes when every member joins the mission, refusing to rest until all experience the inheritance of God's promise. Faithful hearts don't sit on the sidelines—they cross the river together.

3. Faithfulness transforms compromise into commitment

The agreement between Moses and the eastern tribes shows that God can sanctify imperfect desires. Reuben and Gad began with self-centered motives, yet through dialogue, repentance, and renewed commitment, their request became an act of service. God often reshapes our ambitions rather than rejects them. The key is submission. When we allow God's mission to govern our personal plans, even compromise can become cooperation. The tribes' willingness to cross the Jordan before settling their land turned potential division into demonstration of unity. Faithfulness means letting God's purpose define our priorities. Every Christian has "pastures east of the Jordan"—dreams and comforts we'd rather keep—but we prove our devotion when we put mission before preference. Obedience transforms what we want into what God can use.

4. Faithfulness endures beyond personal comfort

Though Moses granted their request, history shows that the eastern tribes later became vulnerable to attack and spiritual drift. Their story warns that proximity to blessing cannot replace perseverance in faith. It is easier to make promises than to maintain them. Faithfulness must last longer than convenience. The same zeal that led Reuben and Gad into battle had to sustain them after victory. Christians today must remember that unity and obedience require continual renewal. Comfort can quietly distance us from the fellowship and accountability of God's people. The life of faith calls us to stay connected, even when our "pastures" seem far from the camp. Faithfulness that endures beyond ease ensures that self-interest never eclipses shared devotion to God's purpose.

CONCLUSION

Numbers 32 captures the struggle between comfort and calling, between what benefits self and what blesses others. Reuben and Gad began by seeking ease but ended by pledging service. Their story warns that self-interest, if left unchecked, weakens unity and delays God's purpose. Yet it also proves that God can redeem selfish motives when we yield them to his mission. Faithfulness is never passive—it joins the battle, carries the burden, and shares the blessing. The tribes' agreement to fight beside their brothers transforms compromise into covenant. For Christians today, the lesson endures: our faith is proven not by where we settle but by how we serve together under God's command.

REFLECTION

1. What motivated Reuben and Gad to request land east of the Jordan, and why was it risky?

2. Why did Moses initially compare their request to the unbelief of the earlier generation at Kadesh-barnea?

3. How does this story illustrate the tension between personal desires and the needs of the community?

4. What did the tribes' willingness to fight alongside their brothers reveal about true faithfulness?

5. How does the warning "Be sure your sin will find you out" apply to personal and communal accountability today?

6. What lessons can we learn from the later struggles of the eastern tribes about sustaining faithfulness over time?

DISCUSSION

1. What modern parallels exist to "staying east of the Jordan"—choosing comfort over calling?

2. How can Christians pursue personal goals without neglecting participation in God's larger mission?

3. In what ways can the church challenge selfish tendencies while still honoring individual gifts and callings?

4. Why is shared sacrifice essential for unity in the body of Christ?

5. What practical steps can believers take to ensure that blessings strengthen rather than isolate them?

6. How does this passage teach us to balance personal conviction with communal responsibility?

12

REMEMBERING THE JOURNEY

NUMBERS 33

Objective: To show that remembering God's faithfulness strengthens gratitude, obedience, and holiness for the journey ahead.

INTRODUCTION

A retired sea captain once kept a weathered logbook on his mantel. Whenever guests asked about it, he would open its pages and trace his finger across decades of storms, rescues, and safe harbors. "I keep it," he said, "so I'll never forget how many times the sea tried to take me—and how many times God brought me home." His story was more than nostalgia; it was gratitude anchored in memory.

Numbers 33 serves the same purpose for Israel. As they stood on the edge of Canaan, God commanded Moses to record every stage of their journey—from Egypt to Moab, from miracle to murmuring. Forty years of wandering were compressed into a sacred travel diary, each name a monument to God's mercy. The list is more than history; it is theology in motion. Remembering the past became Israel's final preparation for the future.

Before commanding them to enter the land and purge it of idols, God made them look back. The God who led them out of Egypt, fed them in the desert, and forgave them at Kadesh would guide them into promise.

Memory became motivation for obedience. As Christians, we too must rehearse the faithfulness of God, for the road ahead is conquered best by those who remember how far grace has already carried them.

EXAMINATION

Tracing the journey (33:1–49)

Numbers 33 begins like a travel log, but behind the itinerary lays theology. Moses recorded every stage of Israel's forty-year journey—from Egypt's border to the plains of Moab—not as a nostalgic memoir but as a testimony to God's faithfulness. "These are the stages of the people of Israel when they went out of the land of Egypt by their companies under the leadership of Moses and Aaron" (33:1).

Each location held memory. The list started in triumph: Rameses, where God delivered Israel by his mighty hand. Succoth and Etham followed, marking their first movements as a free people. At Pi-hahiroth, they faced the sea and saw the Lord split the waters. Marah recalled bitterness turned sweet. Elim, with its twelve springs and seventy palm trees, reminded them that refreshment followed obedience. Every place was a footprint of grace.

As the list continues, the tone shifts. Sinai evoked covenant and awe—fire, thunder, and tablets of stone. Kibroth-hattaavah means "graves of craving," a somber marker of rebellion. Hazeroth recalled Miriam's jealousy; Kadesh signaled failure at the border of promise. The wilderness itinerary was equal parts victory and failure, yet both revealed God's constancy. Even in punishment, the Lord remained present. The cloud still led, the manna still fell, and the water still flowed from the rock.

The precision of this list—forty-two encampments in all—underscores divine care. Nothing was forgotten or wasted. Every detour and delay, every triumph and tragedy, was part of the same redemptive journey. The God who led them out of Egypt never lost track of them in the wilderness.

This kind of itinerary was common in ancient Near Eastern records of royal campaigns, but here, it served a covenantal purpose. Israel's journey became a spiritual geography of grace. Each station reminded them that faith was a pilgrimage guided by God's presence, not a straight path paved by human wisdom. Memory anchored identity; to forget their story would be to lose themselves.

Remembering God's faithfulness and discipline

The first forty-nine verses are not merely an archive—they are a sermon in motion. The catalog of stops taught Israel how to remember rightly. Forgetfulness was always their greatest danger. The land before them flowed with milk and honey, but prosperity often bred amnesia. As they stood on Moab's plains looking westward, this list of campgrounds called them to gratitude and humility.

Every stop told a story of God's faithfulness. At the Red Sea, he delivered. At Marah, he healed. At Sinai, he revealed. At Taberah, he judged. At Kadesh, he forgave. Each episode displayed a different facet of his covenant character—mighty, merciful, patient, and just. Israel's survival through forty years of failure proved that divine faithfulness outlasted human unfaithfulness.

Yet remembrance also carries responsibility. To remember God's acts is to renew obedience to his covenant. The journey was not a museum tour but a moral mirror. God had been faithful in past mercies and consistent in past discipline. Both aspects demanded response. The same God who opened the sea also opened the earth under Korah. His presence comforted but also corrected. Remembering both sides would strengthen obedience in the land ahead.

This pattern of remembrance would later define Israel's worship. Psalms such as 78, 105, and 136 echo this chapter, rehearsing the same journey to teach future generations that faith depends on memory. When Israel recited these events in song, they were not simply telling history—they were reentering it, reliving the truth that God's steadfast love endured forever.

The theology of remembrance runs through Scripture. God calls his people to remember his works, not because he forgets but because they do. Memory fuels obedience by framing the present in light of the past. When Israel remembered Egypt, they were humbled; when they remembered Sinai, they were obligated; when they remembered God's provision, they were encouraged. The discipline of memory became the backbone of devotion.

For Christians, this principle culminates in the Lord's Supper. Jesus' command, "Do this in remembrance of me," links past grace to present obedience. Like Israel's itinerary, the bread and cup call Christians to remember deliverance, provision, and promise—all fulfilled in Christ. Forgetfulness still weakens faith; remembrance still strengthens obedience.

Command to possess and purge the land (33:50-56)

The closing verses shift from remembrance to readiness. After recalling the journey, God gave explicit instructions for entering Canaan. "When you pass over the Jordan into the land of Canaan, then you shall drive out all the inhabitants of the land from before you" (33:51-52). Memory now led to mission. Israel had to act in faith based on what they had learned about God's faithfulness.

The command was twofold: they had to possess and purge. Possession affirmed inheritance—God had already given the land; they now had to take hold of it. Purging emphasized purity—they had to destroy idols, tear down high places, and remove every vestige of Canaanite worship. The conquest was not about expansion but sanctification. The land was God's dwelling place among his people; holiness could not coexist with idolatry.

The warning that followed was stark: if Israel failed to drive out the inhabitants, those they spared "shall be as barbs in your eyes and thorns in your sides" (33:55). The imagery was visceral—compromise would blind and wound them. The Lord added, "I will do to you as I thought to do to them" (33:56). Obedience was not optional. The God who redeemed them from Egypt expected wholehearted faithfulness in Canaan.

This transition from memory to mandate underscored the purpose of the journey. Remembrance strengthened resolve. The forty years in the wilderness were not wasted; they were training for holiness. God had shown them the cost of rebellion and the reward of obedience. Now, as they stood on the threshold of promise, their task was to apply those lessons.

In a sense, the wilderness had been Israel's school of sanctification. The journey taught them to trust daily manna, follow the cloud, submit to leadership, and depend on grace. Each hardship was rehearsal for life in the land. Now, God reminded them that the same faithfulness that sustained them had to empower them to obey. The God who led them through the wilderness would lead them into the inheritance—but only if they walked in his ways.

The structure of this chapter is deliberate: verses 1-49 look back; verses 50-56 look forward. The past became the platform for future faithfulness. The story that began in Egypt ended at the Jordan with the same refrain: God was faithful; therefore, his people had to be faithful. Memory was the bridge between mercy received and obedience required.

Faithful remembrance for a faithful future

The story of Numbers 33 reminds believers that spiritual maturity depends on holy memory. Forgetfulness breeds disobedience, but remembrance fuels faith. God did not call his people to live in nostalgia but in gratitude. By rehearsing the past, Israel renewed its identity and clarified its mission. The same pattern defines Christian discipleship.

Every believer had a spiritual itinerary—a story of deliverance, discipline, and grace. Remembering how God has led us through failure, provided in scarcity, and corrected in sin equips us to trust him in what lies ahead. Our past becomes proof that obedience is worth it. The road of faith might wind through wilderness, but it always ends in promise.

Numbers 33 closes the wilderness narrative by turning Israel's eyes from wandering to walking in inheritance. The God who marked every step now gave every command. The same pillar of cloud that guided them in confusion would shine over Canaan's hills. The memory of manna would remind them that every field's harvest was a gift. The story that began with deliverance now continued in devotion.

For the church, this chapter serves as both map and mirror. Like Israel, we look back to remember God's mercy and look ahead to obey his mission. We trace our journey—from bondage to baptism, from rebellion to renewal—and find the same faithful God leading us still. Every scar of failure and every mark of grace become testimony that he who began a good work in us will carry it to completion (Phil. 1:6). Remembering his faithfulness strengthens our obedience today and our hope for tomorrow.

APPLICATION

1. Remembering deepens gratitude

The long list of encampments in Numbers 33 reminded Israel that every stop—pleasant or painful—was part of God's plan. The wilderness was not wasted time but a workshop of trust. Remembering how God provided water, bread, guidance, and mercy trained the heart to thank him for today's provisions. Gratitude grows when memory lingers on grace. Forgetfulness, on the other hand, breeds entitlement and disobedience. Faithfulness begins by remembering who brought us this far. When Christians trace their own stories—answered prayers, unseen protections, forgiven sins—they find countless reasons to praise. Gratitude born of memory steadies obedience. The heart that remembers God's faithfulness in the past will more easily trust him with the future.

2. Remembering transforms failure into instruction

Israel's journey included graves of craving, rebellions, and delays. Yet Moses recorded them all. God wanted his people to remember not only triumphs but transgressions. Forgetting sin invites repetition; remembering it fosters humility. When we recall where disobedience led us, we grow wiser and more watchful. The same God who disciplined Israel disciplines his church for holiness, not harm. Remembering failure should not produce guilt but gratitude for mercy. The past becomes a classroom where grace teaches obedience. Each scar tells a story of God's patience and power to restore. Mature believers do not erase their wilderness years—they redeem them by learning to walk differently because of them.

3. Remembering God's presence builds confidence for new challenges

Standing on the banks of the Jordan, Israel faced unfamiliar battles and opportunities. God's review of their journey reminded them that his presence had never failed. He was faithful through seas, deserts, serpents, and storms; therefore, he would be faithful in conquest. The same logic sustains Christians today. Remembering the ways God has carried us through earlier trials strengthens courage for what lies ahead. Our history of deliverance becomes a down payment on future grace. The God who was with us in the wilderness remains with us in the land. Faith that forgets becomes fear; faith that remembers becomes confidence. Every act of obedience draws strength from the memory of God's unbroken presence.

4. Remembering renews commitment to holiness

The chapter ends with a warning to purge the land of idolatry and impurity. Remembrance is not meant for sentimentality but sanctification. Because God had been faithful, Israel must be faithful in return. Gratitude without obedience is empty. Remembering God's grace should drive believers to remove whatever competes with his reign—habits, idols, compromises. Memory becomes motivation for purity. The God who delivered us from

Egypt still commands that we destroy the idols of Canaan in our hearts. When we recall his faithfulness, we find strength to obey, not excuses to delay. True remembrance always leads to renewed holiness, proving that the God who brought us out still calls us forward.

CONCLUSION

Numbers 33 transformed Israel's past into a foundation for future faithfulness. Every campsite, crisis, and correction becomes evidence that God never abandoned his people. As they prepared to enter Canaan, remembrance became their greatest weapon against fear and forgetfulness. The same God who led them through the wilderness would lead them into the promise—if they remembered and obeyed. For believers today, reflection serves the same purpose. Recalling God's faithfulness rekindles gratitude, renews trust, and reinforces holiness. Memory is not nostalgia; it is discipleship. The journey behind us proves that the God who delivered, disciplined, and directed us before will continue to do so until his promises are complete.

REFLECTION

1. How does the record of Israel's forty-two encampments demonstrate God's careful guidance and presence?

2. Why is it important that the text includes both moments of victory and failure?

3. In what ways does remembering God's past provision cultivate gratitude and faith today?

4. What spiritual dangers arise when Christians forget God's discipline as well as his deliverance?

5. How does Israel's journey illustrate that obedience must flow from remembrance of grace?

6. How can Christians today intentionally practice remembering as a means of strengthening obedience?

DISCUSSION

1. Why do modern believers often neglect the discipline of remembrance, and what are the consequences?

2. How might a congregation use its own history to encourage greater faithfulness and unity?

3. What practical habits can families or churches adopt to keep God's faithfulness before future generations?

4. How can reflecting on past failures help us avoid repeating them without falling into guilt?

5. What idols or compromises today parallel the Canaanite threats Israel was told to remove?

6. How does remembering Christ's work on the cross fulfill the same purpose as Israel's wilderness review?

13

BOUNDARIES & INHERITANCE

NUMBERS 34–36

Objective: To show that God's faithful order secures justice, mercy, and holiness within his people's inheritance.

INTRODUCTION

When architects design a great cathedral, they don't begin with the stained glass or the steeple—they start with the blueprint. Every arch, aisle, and column must fit within the design. Without boundaries, the building would collapse under its own beauty. In Numbers 34–36, God finishes the blueprint for Israel's national life. The wilderness journey has ended, and the Lord now sketches the borders, cities, and laws that will sustain his people in the land of promise.

These final chapters may read like administrative notes—maps, measurements, and marriage laws—but they form the capstone of God's covenant with Israel. He defines the land's boundaries to show that blessing requires order. He scatters the Levites and establishes cities of refuge so that holiness and justice reach every corner of the nation. And he safeguards inheritance laws so that no tribe or family loses its portion. Every detail declares that the land—and the life within it—belong to God.

Numbers closes with structure. The God who guided Israel through chaos now anchors them in covenant stability. Boundaries, cities, and inheritances become symbols of divine faithfulness. For Christians today, these chapters remind us that God's promises do not end with rescue—they continue through righteous order, mercy, and stewardship. Holiness, like a well-built cathedral, stands strong within the boundaries God designs.

EXAMINATION

The boundaries of Canaan (34:1-29)

As Israel stood poised to cross the Jordan, God began the final act of preparation: defining the borders of the Promised Land. "When you enter the land of Canaan, this is the land that shall fall to you for an inheritance" (34:2). The journey that began with departure now culminated in distribution. Geography became theology; the land itself was a tangible expression of God's faithfulness.

The borders described in verses 3-12 formed a rough rectangle, stretching from the wilderness of Zin in the south to Mount Hor in the north, from the Great Sea in the west to the Jordan River in the east. The precision of these instructions demonstrated divine order. God was not only redeeming a people—he was organizing a kingdom. Every boundary marked a promise kept. The land was not random but measured, reflecting both divine generosity and divine limits.

Boundaries in Scripture often symbolize grace and responsibility. To possess the land was to enjoy blessing; to respect its borders was to honor God's sovereignty. Crossing beyond them, whether geographically or morally, would invite judgment. The delineation of Canaan's borders reminded Israel that freedom in God's covenant always came with form. The same Lord who liberated them from Pharaoh now established order among them.

Verses 16-29 names the leaders appointed to oversee the land's division—Joshua, Eleazar, and one chief from each tribe. This act of delegation reinforced communal fairness. No tribe received its portion through favoritism; inheritance was governed by equity, not power. God's justice ensured that every tribe had a place, every family had a home, and every inheritance had boundaries.

This section also serves as a theological conclusion to the wilderness wanderings. The people who once complained of having no home now received precise coordinates. What began with wandering ended with belonging. God's faithfulness transformed a refugee camp into a nation. Even before the land was conquered, God spoke of it as already possessed. Faith saw the promise as fulfilled before the first stone of Jericho fell.

The Levitical cities and cities of refuge (35:1–34)

Next, God turned to the Levites—the tribe with no territorial inheritance. While other tribes received regions of land, the Levites received places of service. "They shall give to the Levites from the inheritance of their possession cities to dwell in" (35:2). Forty-eight cities were assigned across Israel, scattered evenly among the tribes, each surrounded by pastureland. This design ensured that the priestly presence of God was distributed throughout the nation. Every region would host those who taught the law and maintained worship. Holiness would not be centralized but woven into the fabric of the land.

Among these forty-eight cities, six were designated as cities of refuge—three east of the Jordan and three within Canaan. Their purpose was profoundly theological: they embodied God's balance between justice and mercy. These cities provided asylum for anyone who unintentionally killed another person. The manslayer could flee there and remain until trial. If found innocent of premeditated murder, he stayed in the city of refuge "until the death of the high priest" (35:25). Only then could he return home without fear of retribution.

This system demonstrated both divine compassion and divine order. Life was sacred, and bloodshed defiled the land. Yet God recognized human frailty and error. The city of refuge prevented vengeance from devolving into chaos while still upholding the sanctity of life. The requirement that the killer remain until the high priest's death connected mercy to mediation. The high priest's death symbolically atoned for the blood that had been shed, restoring purity to the land.

The arrangement of these cities revealed God's concern for accessibility. No Israelite was to be more than a day's journey from mercy. The roads leading to them were kept clear, emphasizing that refuge was always within reach. This prefigured Christ, our ultimate refuge. The New Testament echoes this imagery when it called Jesus the One in whom we "have fled for refuge to take hold of the hope set before us" (Heb. 6:18). The cities of refuge pointed forward to the cross, where justice and mercy met.

God concluded this section by reminding Israel that blood defiled the land: "You shall not pollute the land in which you live, for blood pollutes the land, and no atonement can be made for the land for the blood that is shed in it, except by the blood of the one who shed it" (35:33). The land was not merely soil—it was sacred space, where God dwelt among his people. Justice and holiness were environmental realities; sin contaminated creation itself. Faithfulness in worship had to extend to righteousness in judgment. God's people had to guard both the sanctity of the sanctuary and the sanctity of society.

The inheritance safeguarded (36:1-13)

The earlier petition by the daughters of Zelophehad (27:1-11) had secured inheritance rights for families without male heirs. Now, members of their clan raised a concern: if these daughters married men from other tribes, their land would transfer outside the tribe of Manasseh, disrupting the balance of inheritance. The issue was practical but profound—how to preserve both justice for individuals and unity for the whole.

Moses again sought the Lord's direction, and God provided a wise resolution: the daughters could marry whomever they wished, but only within their father's tribe. "Thus no inheritance shall be transferred from one tribe to another" (36:9). The solution balanced freedom with faithfulness. God honored the women's rights without fracturing tribal identity.

This final chapter ties the entire book together. Numbers began with organization and ended with preservation. The same God who arranged the camp around the tabernacle now arranged society around holiness. The land was more than real estate; it was the stage for covenant life. Every boundary, city, and inheritance safeguarded the relationship between God and his people. The daughters of Zelophehad obeyed, marrying within their clan, demonstrating that true inheritance depended not on possession but on obedience.

Their story reminds us that God's commands, even when restrictive, aim to protect blessing, not hinder it. Boundaries—whether geographic, moral, or relational—exist to preserve what God has given. Faithfulness was the fence around inheritance. When believers honor God's order, they keep his gifts intact for future generations.

Faithful order in the promise of God

Numbers 34–36 closes the wilderness narrative with quiet triumph. The journey that began with chaos ends with order. The book that opened with a census of wanderers concludes with a map of inheritance. God has transformed a restless people into a structured nation ready for covenant living. Every instruction about borders, cities, and inheritance testifies to divine faithfulness.

These final chapters also bridge past and future. God's faithfulness in the wilderness now became the foundation for obedience in the land. The boundaries of Canaan reminded Israel that blessing requires stewardship. The Levitical cities ensured that worship and justice permeated daily life. The laws of inheritance preserved unity across generations. Together they proclaimed that holiness is comprehensive—it shapes geography, governance, and family.

For modern believers, this passage invites reflection on how faithfulness orders our lives. God still draws boundaries—not to restrict joy but to sustain it. He still places "Levitical cities" in our midst—communities of faith that preserve holiness in a corrupt world. And he still calls us to steward what we have received—our faith, our families, our resources—so that his promises endure through us.

Numbers ends not with fanfare but with fulfillment. The God who counted every tribe, guided every step, and corrected every rebellion now assigns every inheritance. His faithfulness has reached its resting place. The book of Joshua will describe conquest, but Numbers ensures that Israel enters that story with order, gratitude, and trust. The wilderness has accomplished its purpose. God's people are ready not only to receive the promise but to live faithfully within its boundaries.

APPLICATION

1. God's faithfulness gives structure to our lives

The boundaries of Canaan remind us that God's blessings are not chaotic but carefully ordered. He drew lines around the land just as he draws lines around the lives of his people. Those boundaries are not barriers to joy but safeguards of it. Faithfulness means living within the form God provides—submitting our ambitions, relationships, and choices to his design. In a culture that prizes limitless freedom, believers must rediscover the holiness of limits. God's order shapes identity and preserves peace. Israel's borders testified that the land—and the people who lived in it—belonged to God. Our boundaries do the same. When we honor the lines he draws, we find freedom that is secure, peace that endures, and purpose that thrives within his faithful order.

2. God's justice blends mercy with holiness

The cities of refuge stand as enduring symbols of divine justice tempered by mercy. They offered protection for the repentant without excusing sin. Every case of bloodshed demanded accountability, yet God ensured that compassion remained accessible. His justice never hardens into cruelty, and his mercy never dissolves into permissiveness. The balance between the two sustains covenant life. The cross of Christ fulfills this same pattern—sin judged, mercy extended, holiness upheld. God's justice still flows through mercy's channels. For Christians, that means our communities must reflect the same character. Churches should be places where truth and grace coexist, where the guilty can find refuge without escaping repentance, and where holiness is honored not through harshness but through healing.

3. Faithfulness protects the inheritance of future generations

The daughters of Zelophehad demonstrate that obedience preserves blessing. Their story closes Numbers by showing that inheritance is not guaranteed—it must be guarded. Faithfulness today secures grace for tomorrow. Israel's tribal laws protected unity across generations, and the same principle governs the church. The gospel we have received must be stewarded, not squandered. When believers honor God's commands, they ensure that his promises remain visible to those who come after. Every act of obedience—every word of truth, every sacrifice of holiness—is an investment in the faith of the next generation. In a transient world, stability flows from faithfulness. The inheritance of grace endures only when God's people live by the order he established.

4. God's presence sanctifies every place we live

The Levites' cities scattered throughout Israel ensured that no tribe lived far from the symbols of God's holiness. Worship was woven into geography;

every region echoed the presence of God. Likewise, Christians today carry his presence into neighborhoods, workplaces, and homes. Faithfulness is not confined to temples but expressed in the ordinary spaces of life. God places his people as living sanctuaries within the world so that justice, compassion, and holiness might radiate from them. Our lives should make mercy accessible and righteousness visible. When God's people live faithfully in every place he plants them, the world sees that his presence is not limited to sacred sites but shines through ordinary obedience in daily life.

CONCLUSION

Numbers ends with a map—a portrait of divine order. The God who led Israel through wilderness wandering now gave them borders, cities, and laws to preserve what he had promised. Every detail reflects his faithfulness: justice tempered by mercy, holiness secured through structure, and inheritance protected through obedience. These closing chapters remind Christians that God's covenant grace never drifts into chaos. His blessings are safest within his boundaries. The same Lord who defined Canaan's borders defines our lives through his Word. When we live within his design, we discover that order is not limitation but liberation—the framework through which his faithfulness flourishes from generation to generation.

REFLECTION

1. How do the carefully defined boundaries of Canaan reveal both God's faithfulness and his order?

2. What lessons do the Levitical cities teach about God's desire to dwell among all his people?

3. Why were the cities of refuge essential to balancing justice and mercy in Israel?

4. How does the final story of the daughters of Zelophehad illustrate obedience that protects blessing?

5. What do these closing chapters teach about the relationship between holiness, justice, and community life?

6. How can remembering God's faithful structure for Israel inspire obedience and stewardship in our lives today?

DISCUSSION

1. Why does modern culture often resist the idea of boundaries, and how should Christians respond?

2. What are practical ways believers can reflect both justice and mercy in dealing with others?

3. How can churches function as "cities of refuge" without compromising truth or holiness?

4. In what ways are believers today called to steward their spiritual inheritance for future generations?

5. How can understanding God's order in Numbers 34–36 shape how we use our time, possessions, and relationships?

6. What parallels exist between Israel's scattered Levitical cities and the presence of Christians in today's world?

www.ingramcontent.com/pod-product-compliance
Lightning Source LLC
Chambersburg PA
CBHW070153080526
44586CB00015B/1972